55/500 of a special, limited edition
commemorating the
1997 National Book Award for Poetry

Effort at Speech

EFFORT AT SPEECH

New and Selected Poems

~~William Meredith~~

For Niles and Pamela, with
love and gratitude for
your friendship —
William

TRIQUARTERLY BOOKS
NORTHWESTERN UNIVERSITY PRESS
Evanston, Illinois

12·VI·98

TriQuarterly Books
Northwestern University Press
Evanston, Illinois 60208-4210

Second cloth printing 1998

"His Students" and "Journal Entry (With the Udalls, June 1968)" previously published in *Contemporary Authors Autobiography Series*, vol. 14 (Detroit and London: Gale Research, Inc., 1991); reprinted by permission. "Grace" previously published in the *Princeton University Library Chronicle* 55, no. 3 (Spring 1994); reprinted by permission. "Of Possessions, in Winter," "At the Prado," "A Vision of Good Secrets," "The Quarrel," "In the Middle of the Long Friendship," and "Trelawny at Sompting, 1897" (from "English Accounts") previously published in *DoubleTake* (Summer 1997).

ISBN 0-8101-5070-0

Printed in the United States of America

Library of Congress Cataloging-in-Publication Data

Meredith, William, 1919–
Effort at speech : new and selected poems / William Meredith.
p. cm.
ISBN 0-8101-5070-0 (cloth : alk. paper). — ISBN 0-8101-5071-9 (paper : alk. paper)
I. Title.
PS3525.E588E37 1997
811'.54—dc21 97-9679
CIP

The paper used in this publication meets the minimum requirements of the American National Standard for Information Sciences—Permanence of Paper for Printed Library Materials, ANSI Z39.48-1984.

For Richard Harteis and Michael Collier

Contents

From *The Cheer* (1980)

Foreword

What separates William Meredith from other poets of his generation, such as Robert Lowell, John Berryman, Howard Nemerov, and James Merrill, is his belief that "poetry and experience should have an exact ratio." For him this ratio speaks to the seriousness of the lyric. In a Spring 1985 *Paris Review* interview he says, "I wait until the poems seem addressed not to 'Occupant' but to 'William Meredith.' And it doesn't happen a lot." John Crowe Ransom and Philip Larkin are the poets Meredith invokes in praise of his parsimonious muse. Nevertheless, *Effort at Speech* is strong evidence that in a lifetime of writing Meredith had the luck of generous visits from his muse. His first book, *Love Letter from an Impossible Land* (1944), was chosen by Archibald MacLeish for the Yale Series of Younger Poets prize. In his foreword MacLeish points to an aspect of Meredith's poems that rings true throughout his oeuvre and stands as much for the man as for the work: "[The poems] give the sense of having *seen,* of having been present, which a man's face sometimes gives, returning. They have the quality of reticence and yet of communication, almost unwilling communication." What the poems have *seen* is the Second World War, which was the young Meredith's first purview as a writer. Later his poems preside over equally difficult events of human experience, such as the suicides and early deaths of his friends. More than forty years after *Love Letter* was published, Meredith's *Partial Accounts: New and Selected Poems* received the Pulitzer Prize for 1988. In between those two books, Meredith published six other volumes of poems, a highly acclaimed translation of Apollinaire's *Alcools,* a collection of essays, and an edition of Shelley's poetry. He has served as a member of the National Institute of Arts and Letters and as a chancellor of the Academy of American Poets for more than thirty years. From 1978 to 1980 he served as the poetry consultant to the Library of Congress. Meredith taught at Connecticut College for nearly thirty years.

In 1973 when I first met William Meredith at Connecticut

College, where I had enrolled as an undergraduate, he was putting the finishing touches on a short, book-length poem, *Hazard, the Painter* (1975), and was worried the poem's "free verse was going to be the end of [him]." *Hazard, the Painter* is a sequence about a modest visual artist who finds his belief in manners and decorum is at odds with the fashionable and dangerous pessimism infecting the times. The urbane, witty, but earnest Hazard—a Meredith alter ego—is meant to continue the long-running argument Meredith had enjoined with his generation, the poets of suicide and confessionalism. By the late 1970s this had devolved into an argument with himself, since many of the principals were no longer around. "Friends making off ahead of time / on their own, I call that willful, John, / but that's not judgment, only argument / such as we've had before" is how he phrases it in "In Loving Memory of the Late Author of *Dream Songs*," from *The Cheer* (1980). Although Meredith was fearful of Hazard's free verse, all of the poems are written with the unerring control that earned him a reputation for being one of his generation's most elegant metricists.

William Meredith was most influenced by Robert Frost and W. H. Auden (see "In Memory of Robert Frost" and "Talking Back (To W. H. Auden)"). In 1940, while at Princeton, Meredith wrote his senior essay on Frost and traveled to New England to meet the revered poet. Auden he met in New York City in the 1950s through a shared love of opera. When Meredith became a faculty member of the Bread Loaf School of English in the late 1950s, he enjoyed a deep friendship with Frost. In 1961 the older poet invited the younger to accompany him on a reading tour to the West Coast. Similarly, his friendship with Auden was such that when Auden died in 1973 Meredith was named an executor of his estate. Meredith discovered in Frost the metaphoric power inherent in the natural world, especially with regard to plants and trees. But from both Auden and Frost Meredith learned about wit and playfulness, and the sly ways in which poetic conventions could be renewed through colloquial language. Although Meredith enjoyed special relationships with Frost and Auden—two of the "high ones," as he likes to characterize them—the truth is that many poets of his generation were influenced by them. A more unique influence on Meredith was Muriel Rukeyser. "She was the first poet that I knew personally," he told the *Paris Review*. "I knew her when I was still an undergraduate. She was a very amazing human being and any traces of honesty in my life come from having seen how beautifully honest she was in administering her life and her poetry without any separation—you couldn't get a knife between the two things with her. The real influence was her human model of what a poet could be."

The human model of what a poet could be is what I always encounter in the work and person of William Meredith. "Character" is what Robert Lowell called it. Hazard tells us that he's "gnawed by a vision of rightness / that no one else seems to see," and he's "in charge of morale / in a morbid time." I don't think there is an American poet alive who understands, the way Meredith understands, the responsibility a poet has to "administer spiritual vision" to society. Contemporary poets in general do not see themselves as having this responsibility, and if they do it's often a loyalty to anarchy. Or their spiritualism carries the scent of snake oil and pretension. Pretension—spiritual, literary, or intellectual—is something Meredith does not abide, for it is a misrepresentation and distortion of one's self, an inaccurate response. Accuracy of response, which Meredith judges by how well we pay attention to our experience, is the litmus test for authenticity of self.

In a recent exhibition of William Meredith's papers at the Connecticut College library, the letters from his friends Robert Lowell, John Berryman, Maxine Kumin, Robert Penn Warren, and James Merrill attest to their authors' genuine regard for Meredith's work. "I have loved your poems for 40 years," Merrill wrote in 1988. What is also clear from the letters is the correspondents' trust in the fairness of his critical intelligence, which they regularly sought by sending new work to him for his opinion. The letters show that while Meredith's generation was decimated by spiritual malaise—"dread recidivism" is what he calls Berryman's affliction—they relied on his "vision of rightness" as ballast to their own difficult fathomings.

Meredith did not argue his peers away from their unremitting darkness. Instead he provided an antidote to the age's recidivistic temperament. "What can a man do / but bear witness?" Hazard asks. "And what has he got to tell? / Only the shaped things he's seen—a few things made by men, / a galaxy made well." Meredith's optimism is not facile, however. It carries with it the knowledge that "we are all relicts, of some great joy, wearing black" ("In Loving Memory of the Late Author of *Dream Songs*"). Meredith's belief in his own vision of things is embedded in his faith that when words are used accurately to describe experience they cannot lie or bear false witness. In "The cheer" he writes, "Words addressing evil won't turn evil back / but they can give heart. / The cheer is hidden in right words." Right words are born in courage, which results from our struggle to make sense of our various predicaments. Cheer is what words are "trying to tell us, /. . . It's native to the words, / and what they want us always to know, / even when it seems quite impossible to do."

In 1983, at the age of sixty-four, William Meredith suffered a stroke that left him with expressive aphasia, which means that for the past fourteen years he has not been able to use language to say or write exactly what he wants to say. "I know it!" he will utter with force, "but *I* can't say the words!" Trapped, as it were, inside his body, which has profoundly betrayed him, for the past decade and a half Meredith has remained occupied with the poet's struggle—the struggle to speak. *Effort at Speech* is more than an apt title for this collection of his poems. (Coincidentally, the title poem, written in the 1960s, is dedicated to Muriel Rukeyser.) It serves not only as an emblem of his present daily effort to find the "right words," but it describes what he committed himself to very early on. In the envoi to his second book, *Ships and Other Figures* (1948), he wrote, as a lieutenant in the Navy, "Go, little book. If anybody asks / Why I add poems to a time like this, / Tell how the comeliness I can't take in / Of ships and other figures of content / Compels me still until I give them names." The names of things are what William Meredith has been giving us in his poems for more than fifty years. It is equally true, as he said of Rukeyser, that there is no separation between Meredith's life and his poetry. You can't get a knife between the two things. "Not so! Not true at all!" Meredith will protest. But it is true. We have these poems as proof.

Michael Collier
Bread Loaf
Ripton, Vermont

From *Love Letter from an Impossible Land* (1944)

A Kodiak Poem

Precipitous is the shape and stance of the spruce
Pressed against the mountains in gestures of height,
Pleasing to Poussin the white, repetitious peaks.

Fonder mountains surely curl around your homeland,
Fondle the home farms with a warmer green;
Follow these hills for cold only, or for fool's gold.

Easy winds sweep lengthwise along the known places,
Essay brittle windows and are turned away;
Eskimo houses had seal-gut windows that the east wind drummed.

A fish people now, once fur hunters and fierce,
Fire-needing, they buried their dead with faggots,
And when a man went to their hell, he froze.

Remembering the lands before but much more real,
Look where aloft, you cannot say how except rarely,
The raven, rich in allusion, rides alone.

In Memoriam Stratton Christensen

Laughing young man and fiercest against sham,
    Then you have stayed at sea, at feckless sea,
    With a single angry curiosity
Savoring fear and faith and speckled foam?
A salt end to what was sweet begun:
    Twenty-four years and your integrity
    And already a certain number touched like me
With a humor and a hardness from the sun.

Without laughter we have spent your wit
    In an unwitnessed fight at sea, perhaps not won,
    And whether wisely we will never know;
But like Milton's friend's, to them that hear of it,
    Your death is a puzzler that will tease them on
    Reckless out on the thin, important floe.

Navy Field

Limped out of the hot sky a hurt plane,
Held off, held off, whirring pretty pigeon,
Hit then and scuttled to a crooked stop.
The stranger pilot who emerged—this was the seashore,
War came suddenly here—talked to the still mechanics
Who nodded gravely. Flak had done it, he said,
From an enemy ship attacked.
                    They wheeled it with love
Into the dark hangar's mouth and tended it.
Coffee and cake for the pilot then who sat alone
In the restaurant, reading the numbered sheets
That tell about weather.
                    After, toward dusk,
Mended the stranger plane went back to the sky.
His curly-headed picture, and mother's and medal's pictures
Were all we knew of him after he rose again,
Those few electric jewels against the moth and whining sky.

Myself, Rousseau, a Few Others

From the boy's identification
The playground difference functions,
And hesitancy here
Marks surely as tow hair
Or unnatural height from glands,
Sets the peculiar bonds.

The earliest comparing
Disclosed the need for choosing,
Where the rest played and fought;
Even the collective sport
Became only imitation
Of others' spontaneous action.

Choosing is the full-grown gland
Yet to tell it to most were unkind
(Like the off-color joke
Told to a hunchback),
Provoking a desire
For what they cannot share.

This is the daily luxury
Which alone can rouse us early
And kisses us off to work;
And to this at night
We return with promises
Until the last choice passes.

A Metaphysical Sonnet

More concert than the quick have, have the dead
   Whose centripetal journeys are as one,
   While we yearn to the several quarters of the sun,
And the moon besides, and the stars, are in our heads.

And how do we follow whither we are led?
   Not like the dead, whom gravity alone
   Moves as a unit, heart and hand and tongue,
But partially, now this, now that ahead:
   Against the thing not willed, the act is done,
Against the thing undone, the words are said.

This is a stuff that cannot come to rest
   For it owns ties to heaven and to the ground;
While there are achings in the lodestone flesh
   Still will the quick move out and the dead move down.

Winter Song

Of course across the winter wood
  Love comes through the branches;
Cold converts from soft to hard
  And ache and chirp the birches.

But still the sky comes on and still
  The water smiles regardless
As it holds arrested in the well
  Like a rich woman, childless.

Winter love is love at sight
  With no thing carried over,
Each in the white sufficient light
  Has looked upon the other;

And who would wish the wood to Spring?
  Summer spoil the season!
Love in the winter wood has stung
  And stiffens like a poison.

Quartet in F Major

Great Beethoven, you trouble me this watchful night
    singing again again how sweet it is
this freedom, how wild it is this fight,
    singing how cunning are these enemies.

Like a white northland, icy-white and flying
    are the aspirations that scrape these chill strings,
and are not tune nor harmony nor a wild sighing,
    but strings only that hope, having known singing.

Taut strings, by whom were you taught this wisdom
    that returns on itself with such insistence
and urges love and singing for a kingdom?
    I have heard the single answer of the instruments:
Beethoven, Beethoven only among ghosts
instructs the four strings, haunts my night-strange post.

Notes for an Elegy

The alternative to flying is cowardice,
And what is said against it excuses, excuses;
Its want was always heavy in those men's bodies
Who foresaw it in some detail; and failing that,
The rest were shown through its skyey heats and eases
In sleep, awoke uncertain whether their waking cry
Had been falling fear only, or love and falling fear.
When the sudden way was shown, its possibility
In terms of the familiar at last shown,
(How absurdly simple the principle after all!)
Any tyrant should have sensed it was controversial:
Instrument of freedom; rights, not Wrights;
Danger should never be given out publicly.
The men could easily have been disposed of,
They and their fragile vehicle. Then the sky
Would perhaps have darkened, earth shaken, nothing more.
In practice the martyrdom has been quiet, statistical,
A fair price. This is what airmen believe.

The transition to battle was smooth from here.
Who resents one bond resents another,
And who has unshouldered earth-restraining hand
Is not likely to hear out more reasonable tyrannies.

The woods where he died were dark even at sunup,
Oak and long-needle pine that had come together
Earlier, and waited for the event at the field's edge.
At sunset when the sky behind was gay
One had seen the lugubrious shapes of the trees,
Bronze and terrible, but had never known the reason,
Never thought they were waiting for someone in particular.
They took him at night, when they were at their darkest.

How they at last convinced him is not known:
The crafty engine would not fall for their softness,
(Oh, where were you then, six hundred cunning horses?)
In the end it had torn hungrily through the brush

To lie alone in the desired clearing. Nor the wings;
(And you, with your wide silver margin of safety?)
They were for the field, surely, where they so often
Had eased their load to ground. No, the invitation
Must have been sent to the aviator in person:
Perhaps a sly suggestion of carelessness,
A whispered invitation perhaps to death.

He was not badly disfigured compared to some,
But even a little stream of blood where death is
Will whimper across a forest floor,
Run through that whole forest shouting.

Him now unpersoned, warm, and quite informal,
Dead as alive, raise softly sober interns;
Lift gently, God, this wholly airborne one.
Leads out all his life to this violent wood.

Note that he had not fought one public battle,
Met any fascist with his skill, but died
As it were in bed, the waste conspicuous;
This is a costly wreck and costly to happen on:
Praise and humility sound through its siren shrieks,
And dedication follows in car.

The morning came up foolish with pink clouds
To say that God counts ours a cunning time,
Our losses part of an old secret, somehow no loss.

June: Dutch Harbor

To Charles Shain

In June, which is still June here, but once removed
From other Junes, chill beardless high-voiced cousin season,
The turf slides grow to an emerald green.
There between the white-and-black of the snow and ash,
Between the weak blue of the rare sky
Or the milkwhite languid gestures of the fog,
And the all-the-time wicked terminal sea,
There, there, like patches of green neon,
See it is June with the turf slides.

Where the snow streams crease the fields darkly
The rite of flowers is observed, and because it is a new land
There is no great regard to precedent:
Violets the size of pansies, the huge anemone,
Sea-wishing lupine that totters to the brink;
Others are: wild geranium, flag, cranberry, a kind of buttercup.
In the morning sandpipers stumble on the steel mats,
Sparrows sing on the gun, faraway eagles are like eagles.
On the map it says, The Entire Aleutian Chain Is a Bird Sanctuary,
And below, Military Reservation: This Airspace To Be Flown Over
Only by Authority of the Secretary of the Navy.

Fly just above the always-griping sea
That bitches at the bitter rock the mountains throw to it,
Fly there with the permission—subject always to revoke—
Of the proper authorities,
Under the milkwhite weaving limbs of the fog,
Past the hurriedly erected monuments to you,
Past the black and past the very green.

But for your car, jeweled and appointed all for no delight,
But for the strips that scar the islands that you need,
But for your business, you could make a myth.
Though you are drawn by a thousand remarkable horses
On fat silver wings with a factor of safety of four,
And are sutured with steel below and behind and before,

And can know with your fingers the slightest unbalance of forces,
Your mission is smaller than Siegfried's, lighter than Tristan's,
And there is about it a certain undignified haste.
Even with flaps there is a safe minimum;
Below that the bottom is likely to drop out.

Some of the soldiers pressed flowers in June, indicating faith;
The one who knew all about birds spun in that month.
It is hard to keep your mind on war, with all that green.

For Air Heroes

I sing them spiraling in flame,
Them gliding, all fuel spent,
Checked by no opening silk plume:
The dedicated and the dead,
Themselves quite lost,
Articulate at last;

Sing them telling what they meant,
No small repeated dream,
As public and grandiose their want
As their last lowering scene:
Burning, dropping host,
Articulate at last;

And sing them making purchases
Beyond our furthest means,
Themselves the greatly valued pledges;
Oh, let the contract somehow be redeemed!
They speak for most,
Articulate at last.

Airman's Virtue

After Herbert

High plane for whom the winds incline,
Who own but to your own recall,
There is a flaw in your design
For you must fall.

High cloud whose proud and angry stuff
Rose up in heat against earth's thrall,
The nodding law has time enough
To wait your fall.

High sky, full of high shapes and vapors,
Against whose vault nothing is tall,
It is written that your torch and tapers
Headlong shall fall.

Only an outward-aching soul
Can hold in high disdain these ties
And fixing on a farther pole
Will sheerly rise.

Ten-Day Leave

To my parents

House that holds me, household that I hold dear,
  Woman and man at the doorway, come what will
Hospitable, more than you know I enter here,
  In retreat, in laughter, in the need of your love still.

More perhaps than you fancy, fancy finds
  This room with books and answers in the walls;
I have continual reference to the lines
  I learned here early, later readings false.

More than you dream, I wake from a special dream
  To nothing but remorse for miles around,
And steady my bed at this unchanging scene
  When the changing dogs dispute a stranger town.

Oh, identity is a traveling-piece with some,
But here is what calls me, here what I call home.

From *Ships and Other Figures* (1948)

Envoi

Go, little book. If anybody asks
Why I add poems to a time like this,
Tell how the comeliness I can't take in
Of ships and other figures of content
Compels me still until I give them names;
And how I give them names impatiently,
As who should pull up roses by the roots
That keep him turning on his empty bed,
The smell intolerable and thick with loss.

Carrier

She troubles the waters, and they part and close
    Like a people tired of an old queen
Who has made too many progresses; and so she goes.
Leisurely swift her passage between green
    South islands; careful and helpless through the locks;
At lazy anchor huge and peacock vain.
On the streaked sea at dawn she stands to the streaks
    And when her way and the wind have made her long,
The planes rise heavy from her whining deck.
Then the bomb's luck, the gun's poise and chattering,
    The far-off dying, are her near affair;
With her sprung creatures become weak or strong
    She watches them down the sky and disappear,
    Heart gone, sea-bound, committed all to air.

Transport

Now seven days from land the gulls still wheel
High and astern. Quiet but fierce with hunger
They follow the fantail: so does the violin, steel-
Thin, follow a high voice in desire and anger.

Her slow stern rolling to the sea, the ship
Travels with no bird's blessing, and burns her waste.
Bird and hull describe the rise and dip
Of heavy ocean where there is no trust.

I think I know a new myth and this is it:
The strength having gone out of certain old men,
Formerly terrible, they are changed to gulls
And follow over endless ocean hulls
Of their rejecting states, wishing for them
Catastrophe. But we shall prosper yet.

Battlewagon

I see you standing out from the mind's roadstead
For nowhere, as like as not, and moving dimmer.
White and grays that shake along your side
Would disguise you as volcanoes or as nuns,
But although the cut steel pieces of your guns
Drop together like a puzzle I would never have patience for,
And though below decks, terrible with valves, containing war,
You are as baffling as a motive for evil,
I know your profile like a first lesson.

Old Billy-be-damned bang bang flashy-in-battle
Castle not obsolete with turrets grinding deep
Into chambers of oh by jesus noise,
All for one or at most a few battles.
The rest of your years readying you go
Up and down the inappropriate blue
(Because nothing remembered, nothing faraway).
Your crew and tackle exquisite with purpose,
I see you standing off the heart's headland
As like as not for yesterday, and I wave.

'Do Not Embrace Your Mind's New Negro Friend'

Do not embrace your mind's new negro friend
Or embarrass the blackballed jew with memberships:
There must be years of atonement first, and even then
You may still be the blundering raconteur
With the wrong story, and they may still be free.

If you are with them, if even mind is friend,
There will be plenty to do: give the liars lessons
Who have heard no rumors of truth for a long time
But have whatever they hear on good authority,
Whether it concerns Chinese women or the arts.

Expose the patrons, some of whose best friends
Are brothers, and who are never now anonymous:
What kind of credit do they expect for that,
Ask them, or better, ask their protested brothers,
The grateful tenants who can't get their curtsies right.

Finally the injured, who think they have no friend,
Who have been convinced by the repeated names
That they are jews or negroes or some dark thing:
They must be courted with the lover's touch
And as guiltily as if yourself had turned them inward.

If you complete this program, you will have friends
From all the rich races of your human blood:
Meantime, engage in the often friendless struggle.
A long war, a pygmy war in ways,
But island by island we must go across.

A Birthday Exercise

> Why leave out thc worst
> Pang of youth? . . . To be young means
> To be all on edge, to be held waiting in
> A packed lounge for a Personal Call
> From Long Distance, for the low voice that
> Defines one's future.
>
> —W. H. Auden

Suppose I were to take you blindfolded
Or drugged asleep or sleeping naturally,
So that all where and when and most of who
Had left you, and you opened five new senses
To an amber croquet-tocking afternoon:
Strange parasols and fowl confront you now,
You hear their whir, and blazered tenor laughs,
The new terms *shandygaff* and *dead on Joan.*
Grass smell and canvas in the dozing air
Melt in the mint-sweet glass cool people bring,
Parent, but unfamiliar and all rich;
While chiefly through the sky an errant sun
Now flies its certain circle to go straight
Into the endless post-meridian blue,
Diminishing so slowly you can't tell;
Nor will the pigeon-eddied stable clock
Ever say bed- or any time at all.
Wouldn't you know, however strange the props
I set you, wouldn't anybody know,
Strolling the summer afternoon I made,
That you had been impressed in the hard ranks
Again of children?
        But I would only try
The figure for its currency, to see
To what extent these things are general,
Not leave you there, knowing what I know:
    Everything the years do
    Can be called a kindness
    And what lies behind us,
    Howsoever candied

By the memory,
Has for only virtue
That it lies behind.

Perhaps the Best Time

> O waly, waly,
> But love is bonny
> A little while when it is new,
> But when it's old
> It groweth cold
> And fades away like morning dew.
>
> —Anonymous

This would be spring, if seasons could be found
  In everything; or if times, this would be morning.
  We dazzle at this first warm shy half-turning
As at a sunrise or at quickening of the ground.
There leafs along our boughs what would astound
  Old botanists and set dead lovers yearning—
  And yet October will see all this burning:
I know because I stay here year around.

We flourish now like Theban royalty
  Before act one: right now Delphi seems far,
    The oracle absurd. But in the wing
Is one who'll stammer later out of pity
  —I know because I've seen these plays before—
    To name his actions to the fatal king.

In a Copy of Yeats' Poems

Accurate knowledge was prerequisite:
He set the Coole swans at fifty-nine,
Knew by sight the mackerels' teeming habit
And tried to learn whole curved philosophies.
Now sidewise like a dusty stroke of sun
His figures and the figures' meaning stream.

From *The Open Sea and Other Poems* (1958)

A Major Work

Poems are hard to read
Pictures are hard to see
Music is hard to hear
And people are hard to love

But whether from brute need
Or divine energy
At last mind eye and ear
And the great sloth heart will move.

In Memory of Donald A. Stauffer

Armed with an indiscriminate delight
His ghost left Oxford five summers ago,
Still on the sweet, obvious side of right.

How many friends and students talked all night
With this remarkable teacher? How many go
Still armed with his indiscriminate delight?

He liked, but often could not reach, the bright:
Young people sometimes prefer not to know
About the sweet or obvious sides of right.

But how all arrogance involves a slight
To knowledge, his humility would show
Them, and his indiscriminate delight

In what was true. This was why he could write
Commonplace books: his patience lingered so
Fondly on the sweet, obvious side of right.

What rare anthology of ghosts sits till first light
In the understanding air where he talks now,
Armed with his indiscriminate delight
There on the sweet and obvious side of right?

The Open Sea

We say the sea is lonely; better say
Ourselves are lonesome creatures whom the sea
Gives neither yes nor no for company.

Oh, there are people, all right, settled in the sea—
It is as populous as Maine today—
But no one who will give you the time of day.

A man who asks there of his family
Or a friend or teacher gets a cold reply
Or finds him dead against that vast majority.

Nor does it signify that people who stay
Very long, bereaved or not, at the edge of the sea
Hear the drowned folk call: that is mere fancy,

They are speechless. And the famous noise of sea,
Which a poet has beautifully told us in our day,
Is hardly a sound to speak comfort to the lonely.

Although not yet a man given to prayer, I pray
For each creature lost since the start at sea,
And give thanks it was not I, nor yet one close to me.

Sonnet on Rare Animals

Like deer (*rat-tat*) before we reach the clearing
I frighten what I brought you out to see,
Telling you who are tired by now of hearing
How there are five, how they take no fright of me.
I tried to point out fins inside the reef
Where the coral reef had turned the water dark;
The bathers kept the beach in half-belief
But would not swim and could not see the shark.
I have alarmed on your behalf and others'
Sauntering things galore.
It is this way with verse and animals
And love, that when you point you lose them all.
Startled or on a signal, what is rare
Is off before you have it anywhere.

Notre Dame de Chartres

After God's house burned down, they found the shirt—
His mother Mary's shirt; it had not burned.
This was their kind of miracle: it spoke
Of continuing grace, if chastised. The Lord's mother
Would stay on; it was simply that the house
Had not pleased the holy visitor to France.

The town's good fortune must have stirred all France,
The preservation of that sacred shirt
Which had won battles for the royal house;
The citizens themselves whose town had burned
To the ground that night, thanked God's gracious mother
For the special favor that the flames bespoke.

The vast basilica they raised there spoke
Of a yearning that reached far beyond France,
A love that verged on heresy for the mother
Who had been brought to bed in this same shirt.
This is our miracle: the faith that burned
Bright and erroneous, and built that house.

I suppose there never will be such a house
Again, that has the power to make men speak
Of *an act of God,* where a dozen cities burned
Would not; to ask a pilgrimage to France
Of men and women who smile about the shirt
And doubt or know nothing of the mother.

The arbitrary doctrine of the Mother
Is no harder to believe than her great house
At Chartres, copied from heaven, to hold a shirt.
Stand at the transept when the delicate spokes
Of stone glow black against the sun of France:
It is as if the virgin's faith still burned.

Or as if the roiling glass itself still burned,
If you prefer that to the legend of God's mother.

Whatever it is, no splendor now in France
Puzzles the heart like the molten light in this house;
Probably no one who saw it ever spoke
Coarsely again of the medieval shirt.

Sancta Camisa, the blessed shirt of the Mother,
Because it had not burned, required a house
And spoke to the stone that slept in the groin of France.

Starlight

Going abruptly into a starry night
It is ignorance we blink from, dark, unhoused;
There is a gaze of animal delight
Before the human vision. Then, aroused
To nebulous danger, we may look for easy stars,
Orion and the Dipper; but they are not ours,

These learned fields. Dark and ignorant,
Unable to see here what our forebears saw,
We keep some fear of random firmament
Vestigial in us. And we think, Ah,
If I had lived then, when these stories were made up, I
Could have found more likely pictures in haphazard sky.

But this is not so. Indeed, we have proved fools
When it comes to myths and images. A few
Old bestiaries, pantheons and tools
Translated to the heavens years ago—
Scales and hunter, goat and horologe—are all
That save us when, time and again, our systems fall.

And what would we do, given a fresh sky
And our dearth of image? Our fears, our few beliefs
Do not have shapes. They are like that astral way
We have called milky, vague stars and star-reefs
That were shapeless even to the fecund eye of myth—
Surely these are no forms to start a zodiac with.

To keep the sky free of luxurious shapes
Is an occupation for most of us, the mind
Free of luxurious thoughts. If we choose to escape,
What venial constellations will unwind
Around a point of light, and then cannot be found
Another night or by another man or from other ground.

As for me, I would find faces there,
Or perhaps one face I have long taken for guide;

Far-fetched, maybe, like Cygnus, but as fair,
And a constellation anyone could read
Once it was pointed out; an enlightenment of night,
The way the pronoun *you* will turn dark verses bright.

On Falling Asleep by Firelight

> The wolf and the lamb shall feed together, and the lion shall eat straw like the bullock, and dust shall be the serpent's meat.
>
> —Isaiah 65

Around the fireplace, pointing at the fire,
As in the prophet's dream of the last truce,
The animals lie down; they doze or stare,
Their hooves and paws in comical disuse;
A few still run in dreams. None seems aware
Of the laws of prey that lie asleep here too,
The dreamer unafraid who keeps the zoo.

Some winter nights impel us to take in
Whatever lopes outside, beastly or kind;
Nothing that gibbers in or out of mind
But the hearth bestows a sleepy sense of kin.
Promiscuous hosts, we bid the causeless slime
Come in; its casualness remains a crime
But metaphysics bites less sharp than wind.

Now too a ghostly, gradually erect
Company lies down, weary of the walk,
Parents with whom we would but cannot talk;
Beside them on the floor, their artifacts—
Weapons we gave them which they now bring back.
If they see our privilege, they do not object,
And we are not ashamed to be their stock.

All we had thought unkind were all the while
Alike, the firelight says and strikes us dumb;
We dream there is no ravening or guile
And take it kindly of the beasts to come
And suffer hospitality; the heat
Turns softly on the hearth into that dust
Isaiah said would be the serpent's meat.

The Illiterate

Touching your goodness, I am like a man
Who turns a letter over in his hand
And you might think this was because the hand
Was unfamiliar but, truth is, the man
Has never had a letter from anyone;
And now he is both afraid of what it means
And ashamed because he has no other means
To find out what it says than to ask someone.

His uncle could have left the farm to him,
Or his parents died before he sent them word,
Or the dark girl changed and want him for beloved.
Afraid and letter-proud, he keeps it with him.
What would you call his feeling for the words
That keep him rich and orphaned and beloved?

Sunrise with Crows

Seeing the sun rise will not mend this day.
I went out in dark among crows older than I am,
By the sound of them, forgetting their summer-counts
But destined to see sixty; and when the sun came up
Red and straight—that always ambiguous omen—
These crows who had never missed a sunrise
Were badly adjusted; at sunrise these crows,
Neither attracted nor repelled, were vaguely cawing.
Then I heard the vehicle shifting of a world
As sad and various as the reasons that I've seen,
All told, perhaps some fifty perfect dawns.
Now I can not think what to tell the sleeping
Against whom I had taken this walk,
The optimists I love, who will never settle
For a negative account of the famous miracle—
A gold sunrise flecked with crows—
Hailed as a mend-all in China, in Greece,
In a dozen fragile citadels that lie
Shattered to fragments no bigger than a man.

A View of the Brooklyn Bridge

The growing need to be moving around it to see it,
To prevent its freezing, as with sculpture and metaphor,
Finds now skeins, now strokes of the sun in a dark
Crucifixion etching, until you end by caring
What the man's name was who made it,
The way old people care about names and are
Forever seeing resemblances to people now dead.

Of stone and two metals drawn out so
That at every time of day
They speak out of strong resemblances, as:
Wings whirring so that you see only where
Their strokes finish, or: spokes of dissynchronous wheels.

Its pictures and poems could accurately be signed
With the engineer's name, whatever he meant.
These might be called: *Tines inflicting a river, justly,*
Or (thinking how its cables owe each something
To the horizontal and something to the vertical):
A graph of the odds against
Any one man's producing a masterpiece.

Yet far from his, the engineer's, at sunrise
And again at sunset when,
Like the likenesses the old see,
Loveliness besets it as haphazard as genes:
Fortunate accidents take the form of cities
At either end; the cities give their poor edges
To the river, the buildings there
The fair color that things have to be.
Oh the paper reeds by a brook
Or the lakes that lie on bayous like a leopard
Are not at more seeming random, or more certain
In their sheen how to stand, than these towns are.

And of the rivering vessels so and so
Where the shadow of the bridge rakes them once,

The best you can think is that, come there,
A pilot will know what he's done
When his ship is fingered

Like that Greek boy whose name I now forget
Whose youth was one long study to cut stone;
One day his mallet slipped, some goddess willing
Who only meant to take his afternoon,
So that the marble opened on a girl
Seated at music and wonderfully fleshed
And sinewed under linen, riffling a harp;
At which he knew not that delight alone
The impatient muse intended, but, coupled with it, grief—
The harp strings in particular were so light—
And put his chisel down for marveling on that stone.

Godchildren

Children of mine, not mine but lent
By generous parents, what sweet grief
I take from our clumsy make-belief,
Neither fulfilled nor discontent.

From my mock-parenthood I learn
Domestic uses, while you feed
Promiscuously in your need
For love, and all love serves your turn.

The bond I gave to set you free
In childhood was my soul in prayer.
I had not thought to bargain there
But you stand sponsors now for me.

My fantasy is this: alone,
Like orphans in reverse, are whirled
The seedless god-folk of the world
And then redeemed by this bright loan.

Miniature

One of the gentlest, as it looks from here,
Of Persian ways is how the shy are known
And looked on in the matter of their needs—
The shy, the disparate, the merely odd.
I have not been to Persia but they tell
How nothing is too much trouble all at once
For irritable beaters when a shy man hunts.
A forest bird was heard to trill for two,
Awkward in one another's presence still—
Two ornithologists—over and over until
They had noted down its call in turquoise curls
On the scrolls they paint with pictures of the fowl.
In the spiced equivalents of cafés there
Waiters grow civil to the ill-matched pair,
The bald and raven-haired, the strong and halt;
And indeed everyone is delicate
Of their delays, of just that complication
That makes at last their loves incapable.
While in the Persian darkness *clop clop clop*
What is perhaps most courteous of all,
The bold and coarse ride off time and again
To do what must be done in violence.

An Account of a Visit to Hawaii

Snow through the fronds, fire flowing into the sea
At a goddess' will who does not ask belief—
It is hard to reconcile extremities
Of any size, or to find their centers out,
As paradoxes demonstrate, and griefs,
And this old kingdom running sweetly out.
You would not think to say of a custom here
'This is the place itself,' as you might elsewhere.

There are no snakes and very little lust;
Many decorums have made life decorous.
Fish stands for food and hospitality,
And the innocence of symbols generally
Is surprising, now that we think absurd
The Noble Savage. *Mildmercy*—one word—
Is perhaps the closest European concept
To name the culture, surely to name the climate

Which has the ocean's powers of deception
When unrippled. The women stringing flowers
To keep the shade describe a slow ellipse
From June to June, like sundials at their hours.
And people have mistaken toy ships
For the ship to take them back across the ocean
And later stayed too long. The practical
Chinese put ripples in the year with Catherine wheels.

Mildness can enervate as well as heat.
The soul must labor to reach paradise.
Many are here detained in partial grace
Or partial penalty, for want of force.
The canefields burn in fire that does no harm,
The cataracts blow upward in the Trades,
For all the world as if there were no rules.
It is no easy place to save the soul.

And there is danger to the native pride

Of a land where dreams make the economy.
Like tourists, dreams distort the things they buy
And float an easy currency, until
There is no talking to the native heart.
Nightly descending through the baroque cloud
That decorates these hills, riding on air,
Thousands arrive by dream at their desire.

One of the last kings sold the Sandlewood
To buy a fleet. For every ship, they filled
An excavation dug to match the hull.
You can see these to this day—volcanic soil
Falls chunk by chunk into the phantom holds.
It rains at night. The trees the old king sold
Do not grow back. The islands have their perils
Which if you do not feel, no one can tell you.

This is another meaning for *aloha,*
A greeting as ambiguous as the place:
Not a promiscuous welcome to all strangers,
But what is more hospitable than that,
Warning of taboos and a hundred dangers—
Whether to you, you must decide alone.
And if it is not safe to come here yet,
One of the things *aloha* means is: wait.

A place to live when you are reconciled
To beauty and unafraid of time.
(They languish, abstract, when no more opposed.)
A place to earn in more chastising climates
Which teach us that our destinies are mild
Rather than fierce as we had once supposed,
And how to recognize the peril of calm,
Menaced only by surf and flowers and palms.

The Fishvendor

Where he stood in boots in water to his calves,
A kind of fisherman, dispensing with a dip-net
Sullen carp into the tubs of ice,
Was only in a tank on the back of a truck.
Blocks off, gulls rung and fell to investigate
What they took to be sardine cans
On the river shiningly; but who contended
For his thick brown fish were rather wives
With boiling dishes in their eyes,
Women estranged by city from live water;
Where even the cats did not wait for the heads,
The scene was that strong.

While the mistaken seabirds thrust the city away
With a salt vigor,
I heard the fisherman's feet shift in the brine,
The thick fish thrashing away without resignation,
The shoppers, half tame at noon,
Naming the coins that routed all of the cats
And were for salt and instinct to a city.

Original Aversions

In all respects unready for a fall
They fell, our first progenitors, and these
Two traumas still disturb us most of all:
High places and our own unreadiness.
Towers or wells unfoot us in our dreams
Repeatedly. Old-fashioned people still
Believe that nothing saves them but their screams
And that an unawakened fall would kill.
Anticipation cannot really ease
The other trouble; waiting for the day
When such and such will happen or will pass,
It is not hard to wish your life away.
Apart from angels, wingèd and prevised,
Nobody likes to fall or be surprised.

The Fear of Beasts

Pity the nightly tiger: fierce and wise,
He works upwind; the moonlight stripes his glade;
No one could hear that tread,
Least of all his guileless, watering prize.
And yet, the wonder is, he is afraid.
At the water hole, one look from dreaming eyes,
From sleeping throat the feeblest of cries,
Will prove ambush enough to strike him dead.
A beast in a human dream must go in dread
Of the chance awakening on which he dies.

The Chinese Banyan

There is no end to the
Deception of quiet things
And of quiet, everyday
People a lifetime brings.
Take a kind of banyan tree
That grows in the temperate islands
Where a friend lived recently:
With what commendable violence
The shallow roots—as blunt
As earthworms in the dark,
As blunt and as unremarked—
Make for what they want.
At night on their way to drink
They will rend like little dooms
(The last thing you would think)
Impediments of stone;
The last thing in the world
You would think of, seeing the crown
Of pale leaves just unfurled
That the breeze moves up and down.

And the friend himself who stayed
In the islands, his small roof
Taking a banyan's shade—
That life was quiet enough:
Teacher and bachelor,
Hard forces both to measure.
With Sammy, a small white cur,
Who would dance or yap for pleasure,
He lived in the four-room house
Under the small-leafed tree
Where counter to his wish
We said an obsequy.
The water had run in the sink
All night, for his heart had burst
While he drew the dog a drink;
And what he muttered first

Only Sammy the dog knew
Who stayed in the kitchen till dawn
As dogs have agreed to do.
A quiet, temperate man:
We have all known dearer loss.
But I speak of the unremarked
Forces that split the heart
And make the pavement toss—
Forces concealed in quiet
People and plants, until
At some silent blood riot
Or sap riot, they spill;
And this dark capacity
Of quiet looses a fear
That runs by analogy
On your page, in your house, for your dear.

Bachelor

A mystic in the morning, half asleep,
He is given a vision of the unity
That informs a small apartment, barefooted.
He takes the long view of toes in the bathtub
And shaves a man whose destiny is mild.
He perceives hidden resemblances; particularly
He is struck by how breakfast equipment imitates her,
The object of his less than mystic dream.
Sunlight, orange juice, newsprint, kitchenware:
Is it love's trick of doubling? Everywhere
Like those little dogs in Goya, objects show
A gift for mimicry. His coffee is morose.
A clock goes off next door where probably
Someone has parodied his dream; and here
The solemn little mongrels of the day
Stare out at him, trying to look like her.
They leer and flirt.
                                        Let saints and painters deal
With the mystery of likeness. As for him,
It scares him wide awake and dead alone;
A man of action dials the telephone.

Homage to a Rake-Hell

Few people are qualified to grow old.
—La Rochefoucauld

When time had got his hair and made him well-
Behaved at last, as clearly nothing else
Could do, he had the spirit not to tell
What little he had learned in erring, false.
Wracked by his prostate as he should have been
Decades before by conscience or at least,
For heaven's sake, by taste, he could retain
This honor: he did not repent his waste.
Although his cronies had grown, *faute de mieux,* wise,
He would make no virtue of incapacity.
With equal scorn for temperance and lies
He recalled his meals and veneries accurately.
An unseemly old man, surely; and yet he knew
Honor of a sort, and not all old men do.

Two Japanese Poems

Picture of a Castle

Now I am tired of being Japanese
The Daimyo said, after a certain war.
Let there be a kempt jungle in a valley
And from it rise
So that you look through horizontal blossoms
A tall, unmoated fortress where the dolphins
On the gables, tails in the sky,
Swim from the separate quarters of the kingdom
Without thinking;
And with a balcony to every hour
Facing the hills, apart,
Where a sweet particular girl will say the truth
Over and over until I take it in.

At the Kabuki-za

This lady wobbles down the flowerway
To show: one, she is leisurely and gay,
And two, the play of all that gold brocade
Over the human form (there is a maid
To hold the weight up of her two gold sleeves),
And three, what no one really quite believes
Anymore, that she is a puppet anyway.

Pastoral

The girl lies down on the hill
In the grass in the sun in June.
Love calls for the breaking of will;
The young man knows that soon

His will to be free must break,
And his ego, dear as a wife;
His hand is a brown mistake
Lacing him into life.

As blank as a flower, her face
Is full of the meadow's musk
And the shadow of grass like lace
On the hill where she wills the dusk.

Thoughts on One's Head

(In Plaster, with a Bronze Wash)

A person is very self-conscious about his head.
It makes one nervous just to know it is cast
In enduring materials, and that when the real one is dead
The cast one, if nobody drops it or melts it down, will last.

We pay more attention to the front end, where the face is,
Than to the interesting and involute interior:
The Fissure of Rolando and such queer places
Are parks for the passions and fears and mild hysteria.

The things that go on there! Erotic movies are shown
To anyone not accompanied by an adult.
The marquee out front maintains a superior tone:
Documentaries on Sharks and The Japanese Tea Cult.

The fronts of some heads are extravagantly pretty.
These are the females. Men sometimes blow their tops
About them, launch triremes, sack a whole city.
The female head is mounted on rococo props.

Judgment is in the head somewhere; it keeps sums
Of pleasure and pain and gives belated warning;
This is the first place everybody comes
With bills, complaints, writs, summons, in the morning.

This particular head, to my certain knowledge
Has been taught to read and write, make love and money,
Operate cars and airplanes, teach in a college,
And tell involved jokes, some few extremely funny.

It was further taught to know and to eschew
Error and sin, which it does erratically.
This is the place the soul calls home just now.
One dislikes it of course: it is the seat of Me.

Rus in Urbe

In a city garden an espaliered tree
Like Shiva, handling the brick south wall,
Or better, like a Jesse Tree, holds big
Real pears on each contrived square bough.
And in a tub, a yew turned like a top,
Which might as easily have been a peacock
Or half of a deer, in the unnatural kingdom
Of topiary, where the will is done,
Is lovely to the point you would not ask
What would have been its genius, uncut?
Any more than: what did the rock look like
Before Praxiteles cut it away?
Then this whole garden four flights toward the sun
Raised by no tropism, but its uselessness
In a strict place, the humus carried there
In wooden trays. The vegetation thrives;
The laws hold; and there may be a rich woman
Saved somehow in the evening by the green.

Letter from Mexico

(Vera Cruz, 10 February, 186–)

You entrusted the boy to me. He has died
Along with his comrades, poor young soul. The crew—
There is no more crew; and whether the last few
Of us see France again, fate will decide.

No role a man can choose becomes him more
Than the sailor's. Perhaps it is for this
That landsmen resent him: that they do is sure.
Think what a hard apprenticeship it is.

I weep to write this, I, old Leather-Face.
Death is indifferent to what hide he tans;
Would God he'd taken mine in the boy's place.
Yet this was not my fault nor any man's;

The fever strikes like clockwork; someone falls
Each hour. The cemetery sets a ration—
Which place my sergeant (a Parisian) calls,
After his zoo, *le jardin d'acclimatation.*

Console yourself. Life crushes men like flies.
—In his sea bag were these trophies: a girl's face,
Two little slippers, probably the size
'For his sister,' as the note inside one says.

He sent his mother word: that he had prayed;
His father: that he would have liked some bolder
Death, in battle. At the last two angels stayed
Beside him there. A sailor. An old soldier.

(translated from Tristan Corbière)

A Korean Woman Seated by a Wall

Suffering has settled like a sly disguise
On her cheerful old face. If she dreams beyond
Rice and a roof, now toward the end of winter,
Is it of four sons gone, the cries she has heard,
A square farm in the south, soured by tents?
Some alien and untranslatable loss
Is a mask she smiles through at the weak sun
That is moving north to invade the city again.

A poet penetrates a dark disguise
After his own conception, little or large.
Crossing the scaleless asia of trouble
Where it seems no one could give himself away,
He gives himself away, he sets a scale.
Hunger and pain and death, the sorts of loss,
Dispute our comforts like peninsulas
Of no particular value, places to fight.
And what is it in suffering dismays us more:
The capriciousness with which it is dispensed
Or the unflinching way we see it borne?

She may be dreaming of her wedding gift;
A celadon bowl of a good dynasty
With cloud and heron cut in its green paste,
It sleeps in a hollow bed of pale blue silk.
The rice it bought was eaten the second winter.
And by what happier stove is it unwrapped
In the evening now and passed around like a meat,
Making a foliage in the firelight?

She shifts the crate she sits on as the March
Wind mounts from the sea. The sun moves down the sky
Perceptibly, like the hand of a public clock,
In increments of darkness though ablaze.
Ah, now she looks at me. We are unmasked
And exchange what roles we guess at for an instant.
The questions Who comes next and Why not me

Rage at and founder my philosophy.
Guilt beyond my error and a grace past her grief
Alter the coins I tender cowardly,
Shiver the porcelain fable to green shards.

From *The Wreck of the Thresher* (1963)

The Wreck of the Thresher

(Lost at Sea, April 10, 1963)

I stand on the ledge where rock runs into the river
As the night turns brackish with morning, and mourn the
drowned.
Here the sea is diluted with river; I watch it slaver
Like a dog curing of rabies. Its ravening over,
Lickspittle ocean nuzzles the dry ground.
(But the dream that woke me was worse than the sea's gray
Slip-slap; there are no such sounds by day.)

This crushing of people is something we live with.
Daily, by unaccountable whim
Or caught up in some harebrained scheme of death,
Tangled in cars, dropped from the sky, in flame,
Men and women break the pledge of breath:
And now under water, gone all jetsam and small
In the pressure of oceans collected, a squad of brave men in a
hull.

(Why can't our dreams be content with the terrible facts?
The only animal cursed with responsible sleep,
We trace disaster always to our own acts.
I met a monstrous self trapped in the black deep:
All these years, he smiled, *I've drilled at sea*
For this crush of water. Then he saved only me.)

We invest ships with life. Look at a harbor
At first light: with better grace than men
In their movements the vessels run to their labors
Working the fields that the tide has made green again;
Their beauty is womanly, they are named for ladies and queens,
Although by a wise superstition these are called
After fish, the finned boats, silent and submarine.
The crushing of any ship has always been held
In dread, like a house burned or a great tree felled.

I think of how sailors laugh, as if cold and wet

And dark and lost were their private, funny derision
And I can judge then what dark compression
Astonishes them now, their sunken faces set
Unsmiling, where the currents sluice to and fro
And without humor, somewhere northeast of here and below.

(*Sea-brothers, I lower to you the ingenuity of dreams,*
Strange lungs and bells to escape in; let me stay aboard last—
We amend our dreams in half-sleep. Then it seems
Easy to talk to the severe dead and explain the past.
Now they are saying, *Do not be ashamed to stay alive,*
You have dreamt nothing that we do not forgive.
And gentlier, *Study something deeper than yourselves,*
As, how the heart, when it turns diver, delves and saves.)

Whether we give assent to this or rage
Is a question of temperament and does not matter.
Some will has been done past our understanding,
Past our guilt surely, equal to our fears.
Dullards, we are set again to the cryptic blank page
Where the sea schools us with terrible water.
The noise of a boat breaking up and its men is in our ears.
The bottom here is too far down for our sounding;
The ocean was salt before we crawled to tears.

Orpheus

The lute and my skill with it came unasked from Apollo,
But the girl I drew myself from the trunk of a tree
And she lodged in me then as she had in the black willow.
I was tuned like strings: she had the skill of me.

She was taken by death on one of three pretenses:
A jealous brother, a jealous god, or a serpent.
The mind turns from causes in such cases—
All a man can say is, it happened.

Now with my father's favors, the lute and skill,
Through the dark smelly places where the gods play
With the unlucky, I ape a smiling way,
And do prodigious feats of vaudeville.

The meaningless ordeals I've tuned to meaning!
The foul caprice I've zithered into just!
As if my love were no more than a god's lust,
Lend me Euridice, I sing and sing.

On Falling Asleep to Birdsong

In a tree at the edge of the clearing
A whippoorwill calls in the dark,
An American forest bird.
Lying in bed I hear him;
He is old, or at least no answer
Comes from the wood behind him;
I lose him there in the topmost
Invisible twigs in my head.

At the edge of the town I grow old
On a farm, sooner or later.
Lying alone at night
I remember my father and mother;
I see them, not tossing together
In their concern over me
But propped on separate pillows,
Going away like trees
A leaf at a time and angry
At the wingless, terrible trip;
And asking if they can stay.

I thrash in bed at forty
Reluctant to go on that trip.
I conjure nightingales
With their lovely lecherous song—
This is a question of will
And I conjure those silky birds
Tossing the boughs like bedsprings,
Fluting themselves to death
In music that will not cool.
Ah, I liked it better
With the randy foreign fowl
When summer had her fill.
But I am in bed in the fall
And cannot arrest the dream
That unwinds a chase and a rape
And ends in Thracian pain.

Although no bird comes,
The whippoorwill does not mourn.
At the bourn of human farms
He holds a constant song;
When time has gone away
He calls to what he calls.
Dark bird, we will prevail
If life indeed is one—
The fluting time and now,
Now and the pillow-time
Propped with knowledge and pain.
If some dark call repeats
And means the same and more,
The rest I will endure.
If it is one, dark bird
Who watches my middle sleep,
I will grow old, as a man
Will read of a transformation:
Knowing it is a fable
Contrived to answer a question
Answered, if ever, in fables,
Yet all of a piece and clever
And at some level, true.

For His Father

When I was young I looked high and low for a father,
And what blond sons you must have tried on then!
But only your blood could give us our two men
And in the end we settled for one another.

Whatever death is, it sets pretenders free.
The secret loss or boyhood or self-defense
That won me your affectionate pretense
Is in a grave. Now you judge only me.

But like a living son I go on railing
A little, or praising under my breath,
Not knowing the generosity of death,
Fearing your judgment on my old failing.

Dear ghost, take pleasure in our good report,
And bully me no further with my blame.
You use my eyes at last; I sign your name
Deliberately beneath my life and art.

Roots

Mrs. Leamington stood on a cloud,
Quarreling with a dragon—it was May,
When things tend to look allegorical—
As I drove up the hill that silhouettes
Her house against the east. In any month
She's hard to place—scattered and sibylline:
She hangs the curtains for me in the fall
(Rather than let me ruin them myself)
And warns me about thieves and moths and women—
Nothing for money, all for neighborhood.

'My god you get out early, Mrs. L,'
I said to her. 'I don't sleep well,' she said,
'Everybody drinks too much today.
Where this root's tree is, I'll never know.'
I joined her like a knight in his good clothes
And we rode the hairy serpent through the grass
To the edge of the rectangle she was turning up,
But he was saying nothing, by his depth
Or diameter, about which way he'd come from.
There was a row of planted Norway maple
Along the drive, a hundred feet away,
But this yellow runner didn't look like them.
I cut it with the spade and smelled its tail.
'Nothing I could recognize,' she said.
'There's some new aspen skittering in the wood
Behind the house. I'll bet it comes from them.'
She chopped at what was left with a short hoe.
'It's roots I'm putting in, as a matter of fact—
Fat and tidy little roots, potatoes.
There's no room for them in the kitchen garden
But someone sent me special ones this year
From Canada. Let's go and get some coffee.'

Dish towels and her nylon underwear
Were on the clothes tree; straining at the door
Was her Mercedes. It was half past eight.
We sat in the kitchen on her good antiques.

'Have you ever really thought about roots,'
She asked, filling a pair of luster cups,
'What a world they are, swaying in the thick air
Under us, upside down?'
                                        I'd thought about them
All the week before, when the elms were budding,
The twigs so delicate we might have had
A Chinese landscapist for first selectman
Who put out all the town roads to wild plum.
In a week they would be plain leafy elms—
Not a gross thing to be, god knows, but coarser—
And I'd thought how their roots all year around
Would keep that primavera delicacy.
So I said, 'I have, a little. What about them?'

'When I was a girl, my father put those cedars
In the hedge along the road. He told us then
(I don't suppose it's true but it ought to be)
That a tree repeats its structure, up and down,
The roots mirroring the branches; and he showed
Us how the taproot of a cedar tree
Is the same length as the trunk, and the green brush
In the air is shaped like the brown brush in the earth.
Did you ever notice the trees in Fragonard?'

'They don't look real,' I said, 'They look like coral.'

'They look like roots, is what they look like. Wait.'
She went and got a book of reproductions
And showed me the lady swinging on the swing
In a mass of greenery and silk and cloud.
Then suddenly she turned it upside down
And the cloudy leaves and the clouds turned into rocks
And the boles of the trees were gripping them like roots.
'Think of the branches tossing in the loam,
Reaching for rays of water, the way leaves
Arrange themselves for sunlight, except lacier.'

'Does Pluto keep potatoes in a vase
Like zinnias, do you suppose?' I asked.

Her face took on the aspect of quotation.
'"The Magus Zoroaster, my dead child,"
—That's Shelley, the Spirit of Earth in Shelley—
"Met his own image walking in the garden.
That apparition, sole of men, he saw.
For know there are two worlds of life and death:
One that which thou beholdest; but the other
Is underneath the grave, where do inhabit
The shadows of all forms that think and live,
Till death unite them and they part no more."
—*Prometheus Unbound,* a long dull poem.
Please use the ashtray, not my luster saucer.'

'The strangest thing would be to meet yourself.
Above ground or below I wouldn't like it.'

The gothic-blossomed tree of Leamingtons,
Her husband's run-out people in the south
(He sleeps in Arlington in Captain's stripes)
Seemed to catch but didn't hold her eye.
'I've been thinking about dying,' she went on.
'I'll be seventy-four this summer, so I ought to.
Some of my mother's people are right here,
On this place, I mean, just across the road.
It used to be a graveyard. There are beech trees
All around it and a view upriver.
Maybe I'll have them put me there intact;
I used to say I'd like to drift as ashes
Over the fields, and give them that much back.
But more and more I think of the beech roots
Holding up stones like blossoms or like nests
Or like the colored stones on a jade tree—
That slope was never cleared, it's mostly stones—
And in the lower branches, a treehouse:
A box in the ground where I meet my own image sleeping,
The soft brown branches raising it aloft—
Except aloft is down or I sleep face down.
Well, back to my spuds,' she said. 'Don't you hate that word?
Yet it's good Middle English. Stop on your way home.
By then perhaps we'll both have earned a drink.'

An Old Field Mowed for Appearances' Sake

My loud machine for making hay
Mutters about our work today.
Through bushes and small trees it flails—
Blueberry, sumac, cherry, bay.

I lay the little woods in swales
To burn them as the daylight fails
For no surviving horse or cow
Is fed such crazy salad bales.

They fall like jackstraws, anyhow,
Or like the forest, trunk and bough
That harder hands and will than these
Burned once, where it is meadow now.

I side with meadow against trees
Because of woodsmoke in the breeze,
The ghost of other foes—though both
Would find us puny enemies,
Second growth and second growth.

An Assent to Wildflowers

"Ay" and "no" too was no good divinity.

—*King Lear*

Plucked from their sockets like eyes that gave offense,
Dozens of black-eyed Susans gaze
Into the room—a composite lens
Like a fly's, staring out of a bronze vase.

Gloucestered out of the meadow by the hands
I love, they ask me do I know
What they mean by this bold flower-glance?
Do I know who made the room glow?

And the answer of course is love, but before I can say
Love, I see the other question they raise,
Like anything blind that gapes at you that way.
A man may see how this world goes with no eyes.

The luster of the room goes blear for a minute,
Then, like Gloucester, I begin to guess.
I imagine the world, I imagine the world and you in it:
There's flowering, there's a dark question answered yes.

For Guillaume Apollinaire

The day is colorless like Swiss characters in a novel
And I sit at a desk in an old house left to the arts
Teaching your poems English.
I have read the French words in the dictionary starting with "W."
They are borrowings, too: *wesleyen, wigwam, wisigoth*
And *wattman,* an archaic electrical-tram driver.
If you were alive this summer you'd be 82.

The fourth floor of the mansion, just less than an acre,
Is servants' country. For years it was settled—
Chambermaids, kitchenmaids, footmen, a butler, a cook.
Somewhere there must be almost an acre of them now
Laid out in the Romanesque floor plan under the sod,
And the lady who rang for them.
The house is a good place to work. But these poems—
How quickly the strangeness would pass from things if it were
  not for them.

Five Poems of Guillaume Apollinaire

(Translations)

I. Autumn Crocuses

In fall the fields are poisonous but fair
Where, slowly poisoning, the cattle graze.
The meadow saffron, *colchicum,* thrives there,
Color of lilac and the circles under eyes.
My life pastures so on the autumn hue
Of your eyes and slowly poisons itself too.
Children in queer jackets come and play
Harmonicas and pick the purple flowers
Which are like mothers, their own daughters' daughters.
When your saffron eyelids raise and lower
They are like flowers that a crazy wind flutters.
The shepherd sings the cattle on their way
As, slow and lowingly and for all time, they pass
From the broad evil-flowered autumn grass.

II. Annie

Between Mobile and Galveston
On the seacoast of Texas
There's a big garden full of rosebushes
And a house like a big rose.

Often there is a woman
Walking alone in the garden
And when I pass on the lime-bordered highway
We look at one another.

She is a Mennonite, this woman,
And her rosebushes and her clothes are buttonless.
I see that two buttons are missing from my jacket.
The lady and I observe almost the same rite.

III. Mountebanks

The mountebanks appear like smoke
And through the churchless village walk
Passing the door of the gray inn

And off like smoke across the plain.
The children run in front and mime
Their elders follow in a dream
Fruit trees resign themselves to pillage
Once this music wakes the village.

They carry odd-shaped weights and props
And thumping drums and gilded hoops
And beasts with cups interpret where
They pass, a monkey and a bear.

IV. Autumn

In the fog a farmer with a hobbled leg
And his ox pass slowly by, in the autumn fog
That hides the villages, beggared and dumb;
And as he passes you hear the farmer hum
A song about love and a lover forsaken,
It tells of a ring and a heart that gets broken.
Oh, autumn, autumn has made summer die.
In the fog two gray silhouettes pass by.

V. Rhenish Night

My glass is filled with a wine that trembles like flame.
Listen, a boatman is singing a slow song
About a moonlight night when seven women came
Out of the river and their hair was green and long.

Now sing and dance until the terrace whirls
And the boatman's slow song fades
And bring me all the pretty blond-haired girls
With the still gaze and the coiled braids.

The Rhine flows drunk, its vine-leaves trailing after,
The trembling gold of night is mirrored there.
Like a death rattle the slow song grows softer
About the nymphs who bewitched the summer with their green hair—

My glass has shattered like a peal of laughter.

Fables about Error

I. A Ritual Mouse

The mouse in the cupboard repeats himself.
Every morning he lies upside down
Astonished at the violence of the spring
That has tumbled him and the flimsy trap again.
His beady expressionless eyes do not speak
Of the terrible moment we sleep through.
Sometimes a little blood runs from his mouth,
Small and dry like his person.
I throw him into the laurel bush as being too small
To give the offenses that occasion burial.

It begins to be winter; he is a field mouse
And comes in, but how unwisely, from the cold.
Elsewhere now, and from their own points of view,
Cats and poisoners are making the same criticism:
He seems no wiser for having been taken
A dozen nights running. He looks weak;
Given a subtler trap he might have informed
Or tried to bargain with whatever it is mice have.

Surely there is always that in experience
Which could warn us; and the worst
That can be said of any of us is:
He did not pay attention.

II. A Fable of Grackles

Like a rift of acrid smoke
A flock of grackles fling in from the river
And fight for the winter sun
Or for seed, is it, in the flailed grass.
Their speech is a mean and endless quarrel
And even in their rising
They keep a sense of strife, flat across the orchard;
Viciousness and greed
Sharpen the spaces of sky between them.

Tonight will bring the dream of fire in the theater
Where rancor drifts through the building
And at the exit, where the screaming should be,
We will trample each other in silence,
And no one get to safety
And no one yield in love.

III. The Tale of the House Swallow on Cape Ann (Alluding to *The Symposium* of Plato)

A fluttering bird in the first soft heat of June,
She clung to the feathery elm, swinging and swinging,
Inviting a mate from the Massachusetts air.
(Each of us then is but the tally of a creature,
Plato's Aristophanes had said.)

But more than one mate came; they filled the warm sky
With dispute of her. For a long, fluttering while
She swayed in the treetop, alone, swaying.
(The body is always looking for its other,
He said, though it is not bodies alone that mate.)

What she did next made the whole party laugh.
Wanton, we called her—a husband and wife took hands:
She was followed by four males into the dark birdhouse.
(In the dark we would solve impulsively the riddle
That even civilized Plato did not get right.)

There was no quarreling in the birdhouse then.
We went in to dinner. Who hatched those eggs
With her, fed and fledged those little swallows,
Aristophanes? Ah, he replies, the ghosting spirit
Is another, more jagged shape. This puzzle is not of flesh;

Many people in Massachusetts are moved by lust,
Their hearts yearn for unseemly fittings-together
Which their minds disown. Man is aflutter
For the beautiful, Diotima told Socrates,
But the flesh is no more than an instance for the mind to consider.

IV. Moral

What is as wrong as the uninstructed heart?
Left to its ends, it clutches things and creatures
That can't be held, or held, will slip their natures;
It lives to hoard or to protect a hoard.
To school, to school! Teach the poor organ skill
That all its ignorant, nervous will
Does not unpage us like old calendars.
A life should be all gathering and art.

Let there be academies of everything,
That the trap in the warm kitchen yield to guile,
That grackles leave a fire single file
And swallows find their true halves the first spring.
The mind should be, like art, a gathering
Where the red heart that fumes in the chest
Saying *kill, kill, kill* or *love, love, love,*
Gentled of the need to be possessed,
Can study a little the things that it dreams of.

The Couple Overhead

They don't get anywhere,
The couple overhead;
They wrangle like the damned
In the bed above my bed,
But the harm has all been done.
And this is a short despair:
Count Ugolino dead
Was endlessly condemned
To gnaw the archbishop's head
Where the nape and the skull are one.

Not so, these secular drunks.
Dante would find their treason
Too spiritless to keep;
Like children stealing raisins
They eat each other's eyes;
The ice that grips their flanks
Is something they have frozen.
After a while they sleep;
And the punishment they've chosen,
After a while it dies.

The Ballet

In a cage of light, the splendid creatures
With faces amenable to anything,
Doing whatever you like—fountains
Of work or cascades of pretty failure.
With flanks as clean as bone they signal one another
On the far side of a trench of music—
Such breasts and hair, such bold genitals

Until you would think we were the caged ones
Where our bodies shift and mumble
In the dark-tunneled house,
Waiting for feeding time and after that, sleep;
We watch the loping things from the zoo of ourselves.

Yet it is not only their perfection detains
Us in the paunchy dark, it is pity too.
That they must signal that way, like eloquent mutes?
Yes, and a longer affliction of splendor:
That it cannot reproduce its kind.

Five Accounts of a Monogamous Man

I. He Thinks of the Chinese Snake Who Is the Beginning and the End

If you or I should die
That day desire would not renew
Itself in any bed.
The old snake of the world, eternity
That holds his tail in his mouth,
Would spit it out
And ease off through the grass
Like a piece of music
To we don't know where.

Then it would be for the living
To beat the grass and bring him back.
But would he be set tamely
To sucking his tail again
In that absence?

II. He Marvels at the Persistence of Passion

Like black duennas the hours sit
And read our lips and watch our thighs.
The years are pederasts: they wait
For boys and will not meet my eyes.

And children are cool astronomers
Who scan us like old galaxies
And calculate how many years
Before we'll turn to gas or freeze.

And yet sometimes I have to shave
And brush my teeth at dawn to keep
My healthy middle-aged alive
Hands off you where you lie asleep.

III. Sometimes He Contemplates Adultery

I had no insanity to excuse this,
But for a week my heart ran with another love,

Imagined another house, down to its books and bed.
My miserable fluttered heart, you understand, chose this.
Now I am led home—cold, grave,
Contractual as a dog—by my scurrilous head.

IV. His Hands, on a Trip to Wisconsin

It is night. I am a thousand miles from home.
My hands lie awake and are aware of themselves,
One on my noisy chest, the other, the right one,
A matter of several pounds, oppressing my forehead.
It is a week since it fluted the air goodbye.
I think of the path in space the thing has made since then,
Veering and halting; of the shapes hands make
Washing a car, or in the uses of music.

Two shapes it has traced honor this right hand:
The curve that a plane rides out
As it leaves or takes a deck on the scalloped sea;
Handily, handily then this two-pound creature
Felt the wired air, let the two monsters kiss,
The shapes that it graphed then fairer
Than the hair of the clouds that watched
Or the sea's own scalloped hair.

And he and his gauche fellow, moving symmetrically,
Have described one body so well
They could dress that shape in air
As they long to do now though they lie
Laced hunks of flesh on my belly—
Ahead of them some years of roving
Before the white landscape of age checks them,
Your body's disaster, sure to be traced there,
Even so slight a change in a dear shape
Halting them, baffled, lascivious suddenly,
Or folded cold, or feeling your hands folded cold.

V. Lines from His Guest-book

Shelley's houses and walks were always a clutter of women,
and god knows what further arrangements he kept in his mind.
Drôle de ménage, Rimbaud said of himself and Verlaine,

As if there were any other kind.
In Yeats' tower, in all that fakery of ghosts,
Some solid women came and slept as Mrs. Yeats' guests.
We are most our own strange selves when we are hosts.

Here those who have loved or befriended me came to a proof:
They must lodge in my head and in company under one roof.
Keeping house is the instinct of love; it is always a little ridiculous.
Yet it is with no light welcome we welcome the friends of the house.

About Poetry

I. The Poet as Troublemaker

She likes to split an apple down the middle
And with her hands behind her ask them, which?
The other children fall in with the riddle
But he says, both hands! both hands, you sly old bitch!

II. Iambic Feet Considered as Honorable Scars

You see these little scars? That's where my wife
—The principle of order everywhere—
Has grazed me, shooting at the sloppy bear
That lurches from the urinals of life.
He is the principle of god knows what;
He wants things to be shapeless and all hair.
Only a fool would want to fight him fair,
Only a woman would think he could be shot.

The Preponderance

> To me there appears an immense preponderance of virtue and happiness even in this world, wicked and miserable as it is represented.
>
> —John Adams

Headless fountains
running loose,
I've killed some chickens
I've seen a goose
I've thought of people
cut up for soap
but there's more to this
than chicken hope
or the chicken scare
that sells what's dear.

I read, I love
I eat, I drink
I watch the world tilt
I watch the children think:
there's so much to it
and most of it good
that while I've tendons
to lift my head,
like a rooster drinking
I'll nod to God
and save despair
for when I'm dead.

An Old Photograph of Strangers

On the big staircase in this picture
They are having a pageant.
The queen comes down between heralds whose trumpets are
  raised
And a man, also in fancy dress, welcomes the queen
And there is another woman in powdered hair
At the foot of the staircase, acting.
The rest of the people are guests
But caught up in the moment and serious,
In evening clothes of the nineties,
They look only slightly more real.
I suppose they are all dead now
But some of their faces are just like faces today.

It seems to be lighted electrically
Or by very bright gaslight, behind us.
They must have held still a long time.
A dark young man is holding a watch that opens.
The girl whose head is too near
And that old man settling his glasses would always have blurred.

On the landing a stained-glass goddess
In milky Tiffany glass
Is faint where her window is dark. She is faint, it seems,
With the darkness outside on this one particular night.

Consequences

I. Of Choice

Despair is big with friends I love,
Hydrogen and burning jews.
I give them all the grief I have
But I tell them, friends, I choose, I choose,

Don't make me say against my glands
Or how the world has treated me.
Though gay and modest give offense
And people grieve pretentiously,

More than I hoped to do, I do
And more than I deserve I get;
What little I attend, I know
And it argues order more than not.

My desperate friends, I want to tell
Them, you take too delicate offense
At the stench of time and man's own smell,
It is only the smell of consequence.

II. Of Love

People love each other and the light
Of love gilds but doesn't alter,
People don't change one another, can scarcely
By taking will and thought add a little
Now and then to their own statures
Which, praise them, they do,
So that here we are in all our sizes
Flooded in the impartial daylight sometimes,
Spotted sometimes in a light we make ourselves,
Human, the beams of attention
Of social animals at their work
Which is loving; and sometimes all dark.

The only correction is
By you of you, by me of me.

People are worth looking at in this light
And if you listen what they are saying is,
Love me sun out there whoever you are,
Chasing me from bed in the morning,
Spooking me all day with shadow,
Surprising me whenever you fall;
Make me conspicuous as I go here,
Spotted by however many beams,
Now light, finally dark. *I fear*
There is meant to be a lot of darkness,
You hear them say, but every last creature
Is the one it meant to be.

III. My Acts

The acts of my life swarm down the street like Puerto Rican kids,
Foreign but small and, except for one, unknived.
They do no harm though their voices slash like reeds;
All except one they have evidently been loved.

And down the hill where I've planted spruce and red pine
In a gang of spiked shadows they slouch at night.
I am reasonably brave. I have been, except on one occasion,
Myself: it is no good trying to be what you are not.

We live among gangs who seem to have no stake
In what we're trying to do, no sense of property or race,
Yet if you speak with authority they will halt and break
And sullenly, one by one, show you a local face.

I dreamt once that they caught me and, holding me down,
Burned my genitals with gasoline;
In my stupid terror I was telling them names
So my manhood kept and the rest went up in flames.

'Now, say the world is a fair place,' the biggest one said,
And because there was no face worse than my own there
I said it and got up. Quite a lot of me is charred.
By our code it is fair. We play fair. The world is fair.

From *Earth Walk: New and Selected Poems* (1970)

Winter Verse for His Sister

Moonlight washes the west side of the house
As clean as bone, it carpets like a lawn
The stubbled field tilting eastward
Where there is no sign yet of dawn.
The moon is an angel with a bright light sent
To surprise me once before I die
With the real aspect of things.
It holds the light steady and makes no comment.

Practicing for death I have lately gone
To that other house
Where our parents did most of their dying,
Embracing and not embracing their conditions.
Our father built bookcases and little by little stopped reading,
Our mother cooked proud meals for common mouths.
Kindly, they raised two children. We raked their leaves
And cut their grass, we ate and drank with them.
Reconciliation was our long work, not all of it joyful.

Now outside my own house at a cold hour
I watch the noncommittal angel lower
The steady lantern that's worn these clapboards thin
In a wash of moonlight, while men slept within,
Accepting and not accepting their conditions,
And the fingers of trees plied a deep carpet of decay
On the gravel web underneath the field,
And the field tilting always toward day.

Waking Dream about a Lost Child

Misty and cool. Morning. Who are you, with one hand
Combing damp, fair hair, leaning on the other in your bed?
Outside is the Pacific where the sun went last night
And already another one is coming on behind you.
The latch of the cottage chuckles in the wind, you laugh.
The others are sleeping. The prettiness is fading.
You think of your parents—a one-dollar bill and a five-dollar bill.
You see them waking up under the red tile roof
Where your little sisters stay: the one-dollar bill weeps,
The five-dollar bill crumples itself in its hand.
Disinheriting them, you put on your orange and yellow dress.

(Here in the East I stir in sandy bewilderment.
What debilitating rage can I share with this child?
I cannot imagine seventeen. I can barely imagine
The uses of my middle age. I am fit only for waking.)

Now you think, maybe the ocean will know the answer.
You don't think on, as I would, *because it keeps vast,*
Sliding appointments, or, *because it tidies up the world's wrack.*
You are simply drawn down the beach like bright new wrack.
Leaving the door to creak on the other runaway children,
You moon down to the water's edge in orange and yellow.
You are like a fresh joint tossed into damp sand.

'More promising than I, why are you extinguishing yourself?'
I call out from the dunes of waking,
'Do you know what you're doing?'
And more than your clear, thin, 'Oh, yes,'
It is your smile that cleaves and ages me.
Is this what it means to be of two generations?
You put a heron's foot into the dawn-strange water.
Who can help what he dreams?
Mist is everywhere. It is damp in this bedroom.

Fledglings

For Ruth Gayle Cunningham

The twelfth grade at St. Joseph's High School in Jackson, Mississippi

As I talk to these children hovering on the verge
Of man and woman, I remember the hanging back
Of my own fledging, the alternate terror and joke
A child invokes, its claws frozen on the nest-edge.

Fly, I hear myself say now, though they're not my young,
And suddenly I see they are heavy as stones—
I see we are all of us heavy as stones—
How many years is it now I've been falling?

Then two of them, a thin, overbright white
Boy and a slower, steadier Negro girl,
Striking out, each makes a fluttering whirl
And I know those two have already dreamt of the flight.

Oh, now the whole classroom is beating leaky wings
As if flying were a mere child's pantomime.
What a moment it is, what a mortal time—
Is there any plummet or flight as sheer as the fledgling's?

Walter Jenks' Bath

For Rollin Williams

These are my legs. I don't have to tell them, legs,
Move up and down or which leg. They are black.
They are made of atoms like everything else,
Miss Berman says. That's the green ceiling
Which on top is the Robinsons' brown floor.
This is Beloit, this is my family's bathroom on the world.
The ceiling is atoms, too, little parts running
Too fast to see. But through them running fast,
Through Audrey Robinson's floor and tub
And the roof and air, if I lived on an atom
Instead of on the world, I would see space.
Through all the little parts, I would see into space.

Outside the air it is all black.
The far-apart stars run and shine, no one has to tell them,
Stars, run and shine, or the same who tells my atoms
Run and knock so Walter Jenks, me, will stay hard and real.
And when I stop the atoms go on knocking,
Even if I died the parts would go on spinning,
Alone, like the far stars, not knowing it,
Now knowing they are far apart, or running,
Or minding the black distances between.
This is me knowing, this is what I know.

Poem about Morning

Whether it's sunny or not, it's sure
To be enormously complex—
Trees or streets outdoors, indoors whoever you share,
And yourself, thirsty, hungry, washing,
An attitude toward sex.
No wonder half of you wants to stay
With your head dark and wishing
Rather than take it all on again:
Weren't you duped yesterday?
Things are not orderly here, no matter what they say.

But the clock goes off, if you have a dog
It wags, if you get up now you'll be less
Late. Life is some kind of loathsome hag
Who is forever threatening to turn beautiful.
Now she gives you a quick toothpaste kiss
And puts a glass of cold cranberry juice,
Like a big fake garnet, in your hand.
Cranberry juice! You're lucky, on the whole,
But there is a great deal about it you don't understand.

Effort at Speech

For Muriel Rukeyser

Climbing the stairway gray with urban midnight,
Cheerful, venial, ruminating pleasure,
Darkness takes me, an arm around my throat and
Give me your wallet.

Fearing cowardice more than other terrors,
Angry I wrestle with my unseen partner,
Caught in a ritual not of our own making,
panting like spaniels.

Bold with adrenaline, mindless, shaking,
God damn it, no! I rasp at him behind me,
Wrenching the leather wallet from his grasp. It
breaks like a wishbone,

So that departing (routed by my shouting,
Not by my strength or inadvertent courage)
Half of the papers lending me a name are
gone with him nameless.

Only now turning, I see a tall boy running,
Fifteen, sixteen, dressed thinly for the weather.
Reaching the streetlight he turns a brown face briefly
phrased like a question.

I like a questioner watch him turn the corner
Taking the answer with him, or his half of it.
Loneliness, not a sensible emotion,
breathes hard on the stairway.

Walking homeward I fraternize with shadows,
Zigzagging with them where they flee the streetlights,
Asking for trouble, asking for the message
trouble had sent me.

All fall down has been scribbled on the street in

Garbage and excrement: so much for the vision
Others taunt me with, my untimely humor,
so much for cheerfulness.

Next time don't wrangle, give the boy the money,
Call across chasms what the world you know is.
Luckless and lied to, how can a child master
human decorum?

Next time a switchblade, somewhere he is thinking,
I should have killed him and took the lousy wallet.
Reading my cards he feels a surge of anger
blind as my shame.

Error from Babel mutters in the places,
Cities apart, where now we word our failures:
Hatred and guilt have left us without language
who might have held discourse.

Hydraulics

I

A Sears Roebuck pump, it would snuffle
a while in the tin sink, then raise
gouts of the slightly bitter water
twenty-five feet from under the house.
The grandfather told them
that even if you had one machined
in Switzerland, like a watch,
it would stop short of thirty-two feet.
Those are the conditions we pump under,
he said, it is not the same thing to push
water up from the bottom by turbine.
The heart knows conditions of vacuum
where its chambers no longer refill
with generosity, though it still pushes blood.

II

We went for a walk in the woods
below the pond: *chung, chung, chung,*
the ram was working.
It lets the water flow
and when a pipeful is rushing
downhill as it loves to,
chung, the ram cuts it off.
Some of it is baffled uphill to a cistern
where it waits its turn at the fountain,
and the thinned rank resumes its descent.
This is happening all the time, after we turn
back up the hill, whether we are listening or not—
the ram takes the patient water-head for granted
and the guileless water can think of no better journey.

III

How does water know
that if it will climb to the top
of the pander syphon's loop

it will be free to drop
into water's arms below?

IV

John Wesley Powell, watching his perilous
one-armed way down the unknown Colorado, thinks:
a river has three ways to deal with an upstart mountain—
saw through it like a log as it thrusts up,
gather a head and flush the mountain out,
or it can flow by while the oldest sawtooth peak
weathers away to a soft rivering dream.
'The waters are deep and quiet
but the swallows are a noisy people.'
He named the place Swallow Canyon. (June 4, 1869)

V

Then there is this racket of blood
rubbing the little hairs of the ear
against the pillowcase at night.
That is nothing—a tiny meter.
One two, one two, is all the little wheel can say,
though one knows that there is a larger,
and a larger still, and that from the third—
the silent, hardly moving wheel—
a computation is being made.

VI

Ever since as a boy I read Lamartine
I have hoped that my heart,
when it returned to the lake
at the bottom of the world, would not settle and mope
there where everything is supposed to be contemplative.
Now my wish is that it will continue to pump
easily, with the pulse love has taught it.
Terrible hydraulics await us. Against them
you have taught me one simple process
as sovereign and repetitious as rain.

About Opera

It's not the tunes, although as I get older
Arias are what I hum and whistle.
It's not the plots—they continue to bewilder
In the tongue I speak and in several that I wrestle.

An image of articulateness is what it is:
Isn't this how we've always longed to talk?
Words as they fall are monotone and bloodless
But they yearn to take the risk these noises take.

What dancing is to the slightly spastic way
Most of us teeter through our bodily life
Are these measured cries to the clumsy things we say,
In the heart's duresses, on the heart's behalf.

Dalhousie Farm

For the Macpherson Raymonds

Will you live long enough to sit in the shade
Of that tree, old man? the children asked,
And the old chinaman planting the sapling replied,
This world was not a desert when I came into it.
Now, I myself have raised some thrifty trees
And children, entirely from words,
But it is friends with real trees and children who will become,
Probably, my testimony, my best tongue.

Between trees and children there is a resemblance
And men and women nurture
It by their daily commerce. I want to speak for this
And for all such resemblances, having seen
At this farm, in the act of sunrise
And in certain other acts, incontrovertible evidence
Of something too few people speak of: a benign nature,
Ours, mirrored wherever you look, in past, in future.

Sometimes I think trees are best, sometimes children.
But there is no need to choose, they speak of the same thing:
A continuing kindness in our sap and blood.
What we admire in the green world is a benign selfhood,
And in one another, the ability to speak of this,
Or better, to act it out. What is
The perverse impulse in some men and women
To speak otherwise about themselves or their green lives?
Well, speech is a planting, but not everything thrives.

It would be redundant to bless trees
Or children or anything else on a farm,
But once I fell asleep here listening to the dawn
Wind blessing the trees, and it came into my mind
(Maybe no language can relinquish this pun—
First the trees, then animals were saying it to the sun)
To be of our own nature is what it means *to be kind.*

Whorls

From the western shore of oceans on the world
You can see green currents starting toward the poles.
I saw this once in Florida, slow water swirled
In the figure everything makes that spirit pulls.

We issue in this motion from our mothers,
If you could plot the three components: the pains
That thrust us outward to the air, and two others—
As the planet hugely circles, and as it spins.

At night in North America, when they have the money,
The young men harness motorcycles and cars.
Fumes curl like resentment from their running,
But sleeping elders have tied their lives in arcs.

A widening spiral in all elements is our way.
Alone, or coupled like geese, or leathery kids in a bunch,
We own to swirling forces that pull us. If a man's going by
Hardened the sweet air, he would leave a conch.

In Memory of Robert Frost

Everyone had to know something, and what they said
About that, the thing they'd learned by curious heart,
They said well.
                    That was what he wanted to hear,
Something you had done too exactly for words,
Maybe, but too exactly to lie about either.
Compared to such talk, most conversation
Is inadvertent, low-keyed lying.

If he walked in fear of anything, later on
(Except death, which he died with a healthy fear of)
It was that he would misspeak himself. Even his smile
He administered with some care, accurately.
You could not put words in his mouth
And when you quoted him in his presence
There was no chance that he would not contradict you.

Then there were apparent samenesses he would not
Be deceived by. The presidents of things,
Or teachers, braggarts, poets
Might offer themselves in stereotype
But he would insist on paying attention
Until you at least told him an interesting lie.
(That was perhaps your field of special knowledge?)
The only reason to lie, he said, was for a purpose:
To get something you wanted that bad.

I told him a couple—to amuse him?
To get something I wanted? his attention?
More likely, respite from that blinding attention,
More likely, a friendship
I felt I could only get by stealing.

What little I'd learned about flying
Must have sweated my language lean. *I'd respect you*
For that if for nothing else, he said not smiling

The time I told him, thirty-two night landings
On a carrier, or thirty-two night catapult shots—
Whatever it was, true, something I knew.

Earth Walk

He drives onto the grassy shoulder and unfastens
his seat belt. The aluminum buckle glistens.
He is watched from behind by two upholstered knobs.
He thinks: strapped to things we drive or fly,
helmeted for cycling and all the jobs
that peril our coconut heads, we rush
on our wheeled callings, hoping to avoid the crush,
the whooping car that blinks its bloody eye
—no Roman would be able to make sense
of our Latin name for it, an ambulance,
the rubber-walker with the spry attendants.

I was to go to the hospital tomorrow, but I thought
Why not today? Now I unstrap the rented Avis car
and, opening the hatch, step boldly out
onto the Planet Earth. My skull is bare,
thin animal hide is fitted to my feet.
The autumn air is fresh, a first pepperidge tree
has turned mahogany and red and fingers the blue air.
I pick up small white stones. This is a safe walk.
This turnpike is uninhabited. When I come back
I'll meet a trooper with a soft, wide hat
who will take away my Earth rocks and debrief me.

Last Things

For Robert Lowell

I

In the tunnel of woods, as the road
Winds up through the freckled light, a porcupine,
Larger than life, crosses the road.
He moves with the difficulty of relics—
Possum, armadillo, horseshoe crab.
To us they seem creatures arthritic with time,
Winding joylessly down like burnt-out galaxies.
In all their slowness we see no dignity,
Only a want of scale.
Having crossed the road oblivious, he falls off
Deliberately and without grace into the ferns.

II

In another state are hills as choppy as lake water
And, on a hillside there,
Is a junkyard of old cars, kept for the parts—
Fenders and chassis and the engine blocks
Right there in the field, smaller parts in bins
In a shed by the side of the road. Cows graze
Among the widely spaced rows,
Which are irregular only as an old orchard is,
Following the contours of the hill.
The tops of the cars are bright colors still
And as pretty as bottles hung on a bare tree
Or painted cinder blocks in a garden.
Cars the same age are parked on the road like cannibals.

III

At the edge of a harbor, in a field
That faces the ocean they came by and left by,
Statues of soldiers and governors and their queen
Lie where the Africans put them.
Unbewildered, not without understanding,
The marble countenances look at the green

Continent; they did their best; plunderers
Were fewer among them than men of honor.
But no one comes for them, though they have been offered.
With chipped extremities, in a chipped regalia
They lie at angles of unaccustomed ease.
In the parks and squares of England are set up
Bolder, more dreadful shapes of the ego,
While African lichen confers an antique grandeur
On these, from whom men have withheld it.

IV

At the edge of the Greek world, I think, was a cliff
To which fallen gods were chained, immortal.
Time is without forgiveness, but intermittently
He sends the old, sentimental, hungry
Vulture compassion to gnaw on the stone
Vitals of each of us, even the young, as if
To ready each of us, even the old, for an unthinkable
Event he foresees for each of us—a reckoning, our own.

From *Hazard, the Painter*
(1975)

Hazard Faces a Sunday in the Decline

We need the ceremony of one another,
meals *served,* more love,
more handling of one another with love, less
casting out of those who are not
of our own household.

'This turkey is either not cooked
enough or it's tough.'

The culture is in late imperial decline.
The children don't like dark meat or
pepper. They say the mother sometimes
deliberately puts pepper on the things
the grown-ups like better.

Less casting out of those in our own
household with whom we disagree.

The cat will not hear of cat food,
he waves it away. He has seen
the big thrush taken from the cold
box, dressed and put in the hot.

'If I set the alarm clock, will you turn
on the oven when it goes off?' then
she went off to see the profane
dancers of the afternoon. It was done.

The fact that I don't like his pictures
should not obscure the facts
that he is a good man
that many admire his work (his canvases
threaten my existence and I hope
mine his, the intolerant bastard)
that we are brothers in humanity
& the art. Often it does, though.

The cat has followed Hazard from his studio,
  he looks mean. He upbraids
  the innocent dog and
  all of us, he casts us out.

  'There's *pepper* in this gravy. We're
  supposed to eat dry turkey and you've
  put pepper in the gravy.'

The meal is *served,* nevertheless
  with felt love, some godless benediction.

The grown ones have wine after the other
  bottle. They cast out a lot. 'The dancers
  this afternoon were, well, *thinky,*'
  she says. She toys with her glass.

'He is strictly a one-joke painter,'
  he replies, 'painted that one twenty
  years ago and is still putting pepper
  on it, ha hah. Finish your turkey
  you two and leave a little gravy for someone else.'

The cat is taking notes against
  his own household. He watches.
  Hazard would like once to see
  things with the cat's eyes, flat.

Now it is time to go to bed. Hungry
  and alone most go to bed in this
  decline and in all others, yet

Someone has fed us again and blessed us
  with the manners of bohemia. Among barbarians,
  a lot is expected of us, ceremony-wise.
  We rise to that expectation.

Hazard's Optimism

Harnessed and zipped on a bright
October day, having lied to his wife,
Hazard jumps, and the silk spanks
open, and he is falling safely.

This is what for two years
he has been painting, in a child's palette
—not the plotted landscape that holds dim
below him, but the human figure dangling safe,
guyed to something silky, hanging here,
full of half-remembered instruction
but falling, and safe.

They must have caught and spanked him
like this when he first fell.
He passes it along now, Hazard's vision.
He is in charge of morale in a morbid time.
He calls out to the sky, his voice
the voice of an animal that makes not words
but a happy incorrigible noise, not
of this time. The colors of autumn
are becoming audible through the haze.

It does not matter that the great masters
could see this without flight, while
dull Hazard must be taken up again and dropped.
He sees it. Then he sees himself
as he would look from the canopy above him,
closing safely (if he can remember
what to do) on the Brueghel landscape.
Inside the buglike goggles, his eyes water.

Music

I. Loud

The neighbors have a teenaged girl. Below the hill
where Hazard works in an old barn with a stove,
the neighbors' house is throbbing. It doesn't move
visibly, and he can't hear the Rolling Stones, still,
he can feel it throb. Will the decibels do structural harm
to the child's lovely ears, to the brick house,
to the frail culture of Jefferson and Adams,
Hazard and Franz Kline? They will do no good.
He would bring his own stereo to the barn
and make soft counter-seisms of Coltrane or Strauss,
but he can't paint to music, he never could.

II. The Life of the Artist in Capitalist Society (c. 1927)

When he was small, one day he was kept indoors
with a cold. His mother was hoovering the rug,
a new liberation then—the neighbors
still had carpet sweepers. One had a maid
with a dustpan on a stick and a little broom.

Child Hazard sprawled on the hoovered part with the dog,
under the tall victrola. He played
his favorite of the thick black
hooting discs, with fleurs-de-lys stamped on the back,
he played 'The Land of the Sky-Blue Water' loud.
(To make it loud you opened all four doors
and with just a diaphragm it filled the room.)

When he asked her, 'Mother, how do they get
the lady into the record so she sings?'
his mother said, at least he thinks she said,
over the hoover (who hadn't been president yet)
'When a person sings, they press him in hot wax.'
(She was never much on scientific things.)

Shocked at the death of Jessica Dragonette,
he slipped her black corpse back into one of the books

and thought of the heavy cost an artist paid.
Then he thought how queer it was to own
all those pressed singers and a gramophone
and not to be able to afford a live maid.

Wholesome

Hazard's friend Elliott is homosexual. Prodigious
feats of understanding on both sides. It strikes
Hazard as making a complicated matter
more complicated. Very straightforward
on the contrary, Elliott says, who is forever
kissing Hazard's wife hello and goodbye.

In the gallery at the opening almond-
eyed young men materialize. They look at the pictures
as though they were mirrors. Elliott is better known
than Hazard, perhaps a little fashionable.
He administers cocktails, he drinks wisely.

In all fairness, Hazard tells himself
and, *nothing human is alien to me*
and, *the truth is, a great mind must be androgynous*
(*Coleridge*). But it doesn't bear dwelling on.

Politics

Tonight Hazard's father and stepmother are having
jazz for McGovern. In the old game-room
the old liberals listen as the quintet builds
crazy houses out of skin and brass, crumbling
the house of decorum, everybody likes that.

For decades they have paid for the refurbishing
of America and they have not got their money's worth.
Now they listen, hopeful,
to the hard rock for McGovern.

The ceiling in this palace needs fixing,
the chalky blue paint is like an old heaven
but there are holes and flaking.
They had movies here when grandpa was solvent.

Hazard desires his wife, the way people
on the trains to the death camps were seized
by irrational lust. She is the youngest woman
in the room, he would like to be in bed
with her now, he would like to be president.

He has not been to his studio
in four days, he asks the bartender,
a college boy with a ponytail, for more gin.
He stands in the doorway. Forsythia and lilac
have overgrown the porch, there is the rich
smell of wood-rot. What twenty years will do
to untended shrubbery and America and Hazard.

Where He's Staying Now

I look out of these two holes, or I run
into the other two and listen. Is Hazard trapped in here?

I have had on this funny suit for years, it's getting
baggy, but I can still move all the parts.

In the top I can make satisfying noises.
I fill it again & again with things I want.
It does not like them all. I empty it furtively.

It is rubbery and durable, I wash it.
People sometimes touch it, that feels good
although I am deep inside.

I do not find it absurd—is this because
I am used to it? (Trapped in it? Where are we?
This is certainly not rubber or a cheap plastic.)

If I crawl out of it at night, it comes
snuffling after me and swallows me. It says
it is looking for pictures. I tell it
it has come to the wrong man.

Squire Hazard Walks

I

Near the big spruce, on the path that goes
to the compost heap, broken members
of a blue jay have been assembled
as if to determine the cause of
a crash without survivors.

                                        Walking
with Hazard, the cat does not observe
them. The cat will be disassembled
in his own time by underground technicians.
At this point Hazard's thought turns chicken.
It is the first warm May day, the rich
black compost heap is full of promise.

II

Ladyslippers,
gypsy plants long
absent, have come
back this cold May.
Erotic, stern
ambiguous
shapes, they can blight
or prosper a
season's footwork
for who finds them.
They choose a dry
roadside oak stand
where nine beer cans
were thrown last fall
by men he had
thought damned (he damned
them).

            It is with
superstition
now he picks them

up, spilling brown
winter ale from
ladyslippers'
rusty shrines or
garden houses.
Peace on vandals
and litterers,
crooked gypsies.

III

Ho the stones came riding here
like hunters, on their ice-barges,
and where they debarked, they stay.

Before this was a place, before
the dusty trees or erect Mercator—
no topsoil, no cerebral hemisphere
that could hold coordinates—stones.
Freeholder Hazard and the bank
hold the place now from them.

Here's one, fern-hatted, big as a mastodon,
from the time when heroes were braggarts,
who would not sell. And underneath there are
vast limbs sprawling northeast-southwest,
the way country people slept so the polar current
would not affect their powers.

Sometimes he digs up sharpened ones,
flints- and quartzes-come-lately,
flown here on the ends of sticks
by hungrier men, wrestled to earth
by rabbit or deer, little stones
who rode to their quiet on flesh-barges.

And what swirling was in residence
here before the ice-sleds unloaded?
What is held in perpetuity? The town hall
with all the records will move off
one day, without legal notice.

The air that's passed through his lungs
or the love through his head and loins
are more his to keep than this boulder-camp,
ready to move off whenever the hunt resumes.

Look at Me! Look at Me!

Erica is eight, a factory of will.
Sometimes she will home in on Hazard and ride
his knee with an intensity few women
can muster in bed, and when she comes back from
dancing class, she dances. Then she is not his
wife's daughter but Eve's, then for minutes at a
time they have one another's attention. She
begins and ends these games. She gets what she wants.

Peter is almost ten. His electric trains
(the small kind, the best) provide much of Hazard's
fantasy life. Together they build tunnels
and alps out of wet newspaper and paint them
with tedious realism. There is no longer
a dining room. Hazard and the boy dispute
schedules reasonably, passengers and freight.
They have little else in common. Each of them
prefers friends his own age and listens to them.
Only household money is withheld by his
wife nowadays, everything else goes for trains.
It seems a roundabout form of discourse.

Hazard's good mother-in-law has got to be
seventy-five. When he surprises her talking
with the children he understands what attention
is. Perhaps only across such years can it
happen disinterestedly. Perhaps that
is why we are vouchsafed three generations—
they are a teaching device. But for whom? How the
old lady (who is so full of energy
no one could think of her that way) watches
and listens, how the children unfold like paper
flowers, watched and listened to.
In his studio
Hazard stares at the vain, self-centered landscape
he's working on now. It is going well. It
revels in his onanistic attention.

At intervals he can muster ravenous
attention to gin, dinner, and his mysterious
woman, who has other interests. He calls
himself a painter. He has strong visual
curiosity, he is interested
in things. But he needs a lot of attention
and all four of his grandparents are dead.

His Plans for Old Age

He disagrees with Simone de Beauvoir
in her civilized Gallic gloom, may she be loved
and beautiful without wrinkles until it takes
carbon dating to determine her age.

He's with Yeats, for adult education—
hand-clapping lessons for the soul,
in his case, tone-deaf.
He agrees with Auden, old people can show
'what grace of spirit can create,'
modeling the flesh when it's no longer flashy.
That's the kind of lift he wants for his jowls,
let grace of spirit tuck up the flesh
under his ears and chin with a bare scalpel,
no anesthetic or anything, let grace of spirit
shape up his skull for afterwards.

Man and artist, he is working on his ways
so that when he becomes set in them
as old people must, for all that their souls
clap hands, for all that their spirits dance,
his ways will have grace, his pictures will have class.

He is founding a sect for the radical old,
freaks you may call them but you're wrong,
who persist in being at home in the world,
who just naturally feel it's a good bind to be in,
let the young feel as uncanny as they like.
Oldbodies, he calls them affectionately
as he towels his own in the morning
in front of the mirror, not getting any flashier.
He thinks about Titian and Renoir a lot
in this connection. Nothing is unseemly
that takes its rise in love. If only his energy lasts.

At the Natural History Museum

Past a swim-by of deep-sea fish,
cold rockets in a tank of air, tamed
by their right names and their Latin underneath,
he walks toward the cafeteria. It grows dark.
October clouds shadow the frosted-glass roof,
the dinosaurs appear, mahogany bones.
The family died out.

On the far wall, a fierce one rears erect,
his shoulders thrown back like a man's
when he is loved or seeks high office.
His jaws are strong pliers. Dawn men watch in awe
from the bushes this blood cousin
in a world of crusty things.

But the family dies out before his eyes,
grass-eaters first, then taloned meat-eaters.
Some of the bones have been fleshed out with plaster
but Hazard and the guard are the oldest living things
here. Even the author of the comic verse
about extinction, copied at the monster's feet,
has gone his bony way.

We descend by chosen cells that are not lost,
though they wander off in streams and rivulets.
Not everyone has issue in this creation.
Cousins-german are everywhere in the shale
and marshes under this dry house. In slime, in sperm,
our living cousins flow.

And grazers or killers, each time we must stoop low
and enter by some thigh-lintel, gentle as rills.
Who consents to his own return, Nietzsche says,
participates in the divinity of the world.
Perhaps I have already eddied on, out of this backwater,
man, on my way to the cafeteria, Hazard thinks.
Perhaps nothing dies but husks.

Rhode Island

Here at the seashore they use the clouds over & over
again, like the rented animals in *Aïda.*
In the late morning the land breeze
turns and now the extras are driving
all the white elephants the other way.
What language are these children shouting in?
He is lying on the beach listening.

The sand knocks like glass, struck by bare heels.
He tries to remember snow noise.
Would powder snow ping like that?
But you don't lie with your ear to powder snow.
Why doesn't the girl who takes care
of the children, a Yale girl without flaw,
know the difference between *lay* and *lie?*

He tries to remember snow, his season.
The mind is in charge of things then.
Summer is for animals, the ocean is erotic,
all that openness and swaying.
No matter how often you make love
in August you're always aware of genitalia,
your own and the half-naked others'.
Even with the gracefulest bathers
you're aware of their kinship with porpoises,
mammals disporting themselves in a blue element,
smelling slightly of fish. Porpoise Hazard
watches himself awhile, like a blue movie.

In the other hemisphere now people
are standing up, at work at their easels.
There they think about love at night
when they take off their serious clothes
and go to bed sandlessly, under blankets.

Today the children, his own among them,
are apparently shouting fluently in Portuguese,

using the colonial dialect of Brazil.
It is just as well, they have all been changed
into small shrill marginal animals,
he would not want to understand them again
until after Labor Day. He just lays there.

The Ghosts of the House

Enabling love, roof of this drafty hutch
of children and friends and pets, and chiefly of the dear
one asleep beside me now, the warm body-house
I sack like a Hun nightly in your service,
take care of the haunts who stay with us here.

In a little space for a long while they've walked,
wakeful when we sleep, averting their sad glance
when we're clumsy with one another, they look
at something we can't look at yet, they creak the boards
beside the bed we creak, in some hard durance.

And if we're weary at night, what must they be?
Bed them like us at last under your roof.
You who have sternly set all lovers to walk
the hallways of the world-hutch for a lucky while,
speaking good of our short durance here,

wishing our sibling spirits nothing but good,
let them see these chambers once with the daylight eyes
you lend to lovers for our mortal time.
Or change some loveless stalker into me
before my bone-house clatters into lime.

Nausea

In the courtyard of the Brera,
the great gallery in Milan
(he isn't dropping place names,
that's simply where it happened),
a sparrow chased a butterfly
around the sunny oblong
for what must have seemed forever
to an insect or a bird—
it was long enough for Hazard.

Above an enormous statue
of Napoleon buck-naked
they turned and wove like pilots
in a dogfight (he was always
scared shitless in the Navy
when they had to practice dogfights—
once he threw up in the cockpit).
This butterfly was agile,
he could really wrap it up,
turning in half the circle
of the fat city bird.
Climbing more nimbly than the sparrow,
he did fishtails and chandelles,
trying to stall him out.
Over Normandy or London
or the carriers at Leyte
the insect would have won.
Like David with Goliath
(thought lightly-bibled Hazard)
the plucky lepidopteran
would slay the gross-beaked monster
with feathers sleek as Satan's
and metal eyes and claws.

But that's not how it was.
Chomp, and the greedy sparrow
was off behind a column

on the balcony above them
with the emblem of the soul.
Before his wife could lure him
inside to see the Piero
and the unique Mantegnas
(the *pictures*, for god's sake)
he had a fearful vision,
a memory it was, really:
in a cockpit full of chili
with cold terror in his gut
he flies round and round and round
a blue oblong in Texas,
trying to escape his friend.

Nixon's the One

November 8, a cold rain. Hazard discovered
on the blacktop driveway, trying to get the McGovern-
Shriver stickers off his '65 Ford.
The one on the back bumper is already faded,
the red so bleached it could be declaring
Madly for Adlai. It's gummy, it tears.
The two on his wife's car, a new VW
kept dry in the garage, came off easily.
(In August somebody said the VW's
must be coming off the line in Stuttgart
with McGovern-Shriver stickers.
But Nader was right: in collision
with a fat American machine they're murder.

Our battlefields are accidents, too,
human errors like this late one:
we elect to murder, we murder to elect.)

Who were all those cheering on the gray glass
screen last night, loving their violent darling,
America, whom they had married to money?
He couldn't tarry at that feast—when the wine
ran out, they would change blood to money.

Even in the slanting rain, Hazard is aware
of his oilskin comfort. He is comfortably off,
a two-car man. Somewhere he has gotten out of touch.
This morning he is alone in the defoliated
landscape (oh, his family is indoors there,
snug, adapting to the political weather),
the patrol he scouted with, wiped out.
Standing now on the asphalt no-man's-land,
his hands bloodied with patriotic mucilage,
he cannot shake his unpopular conviction
that his nation has bitterly misspoken itself.

1969

February 14

(Valerie Hazard finds on her desk a strange self-portrait by her husband and a note which she takes to be a valentine and on the whole well-meant.)

What you have given me,
in those long moments when our words
come back, our breaths come back,
is a whole man at last,
and keeping me, remembers:

On deck one night, the moon past full
coming up over the planet's edge,
the big globe rippling its skin,
the smaller already accepting its waning
and talking about vast skyey distances.
I had not met you yet.
Aft, the aircraft folded like mantises,
ahead and abeam, destroyers running like hounds,
and the wind.

A sentry walked off
the rolled front of the flight deck,
crying *oh* as he fell to the sea.
Lost in the cold skin of the globe,
he cried *oh* for less than, panted
for less than love, going away,
the loneliest noise that ever wound in my ear.

I think dear one that one day I'll fall off
this galaxy, leaving husk and canvas behind,
the loneliness I'll take with me made whole,
myself made whole, by what we've said
in these knocking moments, oh,
and keeping, as hearts keep
(husks and canvas being little abandoned houses),
and going away so.

Winter: He Shapes Up

Now autumn has finished scolding
with sumac, sun and jays
his heavy-lidded ways,
his drinking and his balding.

Today the first snow fell.
It hung in the hollow air
making space tangible,
showing him how things are.

He watches the yellow larches
guttering on their boles
like half-extinguished torches
as the planet tilts and cools

and the laurel understory
that shields the hill from harm
—the merest rag of glory
will keep ambition warm.

Gnawed by a vision of rightness
that no one else seems to see,
what can a man do
but bear witness?

And what has he got to tell?
Only the shaped things he's seen—
a few things made by men,
a galaxy made well.

Though more of each day is dark,
though he's awkward at the job,
he squeezes paint from a tube.
Hazard is back at work.

From *The Cheer*
(1980)

The cheer

reader my friend, is in the words here, somewhere.
Frankly, I'd like to make you smile.
Words addressing evil won't turn evil back
but they can give heart.
The cheer is hidden in right words.

A great deal isn't right, as they say,
as they are lately at some pains to tell us.
Words have to speak about that.
They would be the less words
for saying *smile* when they should say *do.*
If you ask them *do what?*
they turn serious quick enough, but never unlovely.
And they will tell you what to do,
if you listen, if you want that.

Certainly good cheer has never been what's wrong,
though solemn people mistrust it.
Against evil, between evils, lovely words are right.
How absurd it would be to spin these noises out,
so serious that we call them poems,
if they couldn't make a person smile.
Cheer or courage is what they were all born in.
It's what they're trying to tell us, miming like that.
It's native to the words,
and what they want us always to know,
even when it seems quite impossible to do.

Winter on the River

Dawn

A long orange knife slits the darkness
from ear to ear. Flat sheets of Kansas
have been dropped where the water was.
A blue snake is lying perfectly still,
freezing to avoid detection—no, it is the barge-road.

Noon

It's six weeks past the solstice. What
is the sun thinking of? It skulks
above the southern woods at noon.
                                        Two ducks descend
on the thin creek that snakes through the plain of ice.
They dream of a great flood coming
to devastate this plastic geography.
We can all remember other things than snow.

Dusk

At dusk the east bank glows a colder orange,
giving back heat reluctantly. (The sickle moon
gives it back quickly.) The snake is glacier-green
where an oil barge has lately churned it.
Tonight unlucky creatures will die, like so many
soldiers or parents, it is nobody's fault.

Midnight

The farm dogs bark at a soft crash far upriver:
the ice breaker is coming down. We go out
in the clear night to see the lights—beacons
on the river, pharos in the sky, and a jeweled
seafarer bringing water to the parched plain.
The hollow roar grows slower than an avalanche.
Her searchlight feeling a way from point
of land to point of land, she pulls herself along
by beacon-roots. For a half-mile reach of river
she sights on us, a group of goblins blinking

in front of their white house. Sugary rime
feathers from the bow. An emerald and a garnet
flank the twitching eye.
                                        Abruptly she turns,
offering the beam of a ship that has nothing to do with us.
A houseful of strangers passes, ship-noise thumping.

Downriver, other dogs take up the work.
They are clearing a path for the barges of cold
and silence which the creatures are expecting.

Two Masks Unearthed in Bulgaria

For Kolyo Sevov

When God was learning to draw the human face
I think he may have made a few like these
that now look up at us through museum glass
a few miles north of where they slept
for six thousand years, a necropolis near Varna.
With golden staves and ornaments around them
they lay among human bodies but had none.
Gods themselves, or soldiers lost abroad—
we don't know who they are.

The gold buttons which are their curious eyes,
the old clay which is their wrinkled skin,
seem to have been worked by the same free hand
that drew Adam for the Jews about that time.
It is moving, that the eyes are still questioning
and no sadder than they are, time being what it is—
as though they saw nothing tragic in the faces
looking down through glass into theirs.
Only clay and gold, they seem to say,
passing through one condition on its way to the next.

Freezing

It is the normal excellence, of long accomplishment.
—Jack Gilbert, "The Abnormal Is Not Courage"

I

When the shadow of the sparrowhawk passes over,
the small birds caught in the open, freeze.

II

Surprised in the mowed grass
on his way back to the stone wall
in the cool of the late afternoon,
the blacksnake holds three curves
for as long as I bend to watch him.

III

To know what is possible,
and to do that.

IV

In the dream, I lie still.
Booted and brutal,
their pieces slung at waist height
spraying random lead,
they wade through the dead
for one of whom I hope to be mistaken.
When I wake up, what am I to do
with this mortifying life I've saved again?

V

To live out our lives under a good tyrant
is a lot to ask, the old man said.
There are reports that the swaggering brothers
and their wives and foreign in-laws
are shouting again, in the marble house
that looks down on the harbor and the town.
We know what they are capable of,

quarreling with one another
and in contention with the gods.
We keep indoors.
Impatience and ignorance sometimes ignite
in a flash of bravery among us,
he said. It is usually inappropriate.

VI

Some normal excellence, of long accomplishment,
is all that can justify our sly survivals.

Recollection of Bellagio

For John and Charlotte Marshall

On the dark lake below, the fishermen's bells
are calling to one another from their nets.
Who is here on the dark promontory at night?
Tossed by the April wind,
a horizontal pine, warped to the cliff,
married to the limestone cliff by the east wind,
rises and falls, rises and falls.
And who sees, against the stars,
the needled tufts change and exchange
like dancers, gracious dependents?
The fixed stars are a commodious dancing-
floor, at any moment the pine tufts
know where their home-places are
on the polished floor of the marble constellations.

How long has this been going on, this *allemande,*
before a man's thoughts climbed up to sit
on the limestone knob and watch (briefly,
as man's thoughts' eyes watch) the needles
keeping time to the bells which the same wind rocks
on the water below, marking the fishermen's nets—
thoughts he would haul in later from the lake
of time, feeling himself drawn clumsy
back into time's figure, hand over hand,
by the grace of pine boughs? And who
is saying these words, now that that man
is a shade, has become his own shade?
I see the shade rise slow and ghostly from its seat
on the soft, grainy stone, I watch it descend
by the graveled paths of the promontory,
under a net of steady stars, in April,
from the boughs' rite and the bells'—quiet,
my shade, and long ago, and still going on.

Country Stars

The nearsighted child has taken off her glasses
and come downstairs to be kissed goodnight.
She blows on a black windowpane until it's white.
Over the apple trees a great bear passes
but she puts her own construction on the night.

Two cities, a chemical plant, and clotted cars
breathe our distrust of darkness on the air,
clouding the pane between us and the stars.
But have no fear, or only proper fear:
the bright watchers are still there.

Homage to Paul Mellon, I. M. Pei, Their Gallery, and Washington City

Granite and marble,
women and men,
took a long while to make.

America and the Bill of Rights,
a lot of trouble,
and it's not done yet. Praise be.
It is so interesting,
and lucky, like crustacean deposit.

We've troubled the stones to stand up here
in attitudes of serenity,
our guesses at un-trouble,
what that must be like.
(These are short whiles,
to a stone's way of thinking.)

Meanwhile, Munch and Noguchi
and a long deposit of the sweetest troublers
required this reckless glacier,
these knives of stone, these pink prows,
and among them, safe hogans of white space.

And where would any of us be
if the limestone creatures had held back,
the roiling magma demurred? or the genes?
We've given assent to ourselves
in this city for a while,
laying down stone like our own sweet lives.

On Jenkins' Hill

(The old name for Capitol Hill)

The weather came over this low knoll, west to east,
before there was a word for leaf-fall, before
there were any leaves. Weathers will nuzzle and preen
whatever earthwork we leave here. And we know now,
don't we, that we will be leaving, by fire or ice,
our own or His, or at the very worst, nobody's.
May that be a long time off. Now,
it is our hill for debating.

The dome at the top of the hill, heavy with reference,
is iron out of the soil, yearned up as if it were white stone,
the way for a time our thought and rhetoric yearned upward.
Here our surrogates sit. It is almost too much for them,
some days, to make the world go around.
They are urged to clean it, to sully it more grandly,
to let it alone. We have elected them, they are our elect.

If we only knew what to ask, there are trees, white oaks,
not far from here that have seen the whole thing.
Year after year they have put on new growth, dropped leaves.
I can tell you this much: it is a badly informed citizen
who stands on this hill and scoffs.

A Firescreen at Mount Vernon

When the face is struck
by the nearer sun
in the fireplace,
summer or winter
the eyes water.

See in the painting
of the ironworks
how the ingot hurts—
the visitor cowers
like a bad angel,
arm over face,
the apprentice weeps.
All but the smithy,
toughened like Vulcan,
turn from the heat.

And here indoors
in the gentleroom
is a thin inflammable
furniture,
a wooden rack
(which you would think
in that final access
of reasonableness
they'd have wrought of iron).
It holds a small screen,
some woman's skill,
a needlepoint scene
between face and fire,
shading those faces
whose evenings are gone.

Erect of posture,
sociably garbed,
they were far from the smoke
of midden and cave,

as we are no longer
who marvel dry-eyed
and stare like savages
at this fragile decorum
of rosewood or fruitwood,
imagining people
whom reading or sewing
had fired to tears.

A Mild-Spoken Citizen Finally Writes to the White House

Please read this letter when you are alone.
Don't be afraid to listen to what may change you,
I am urging on you only what I myself have done.

In the first place, I respect the office, although one night
last spring, when you had committed (in my eyes)
criminal folly, and there was a toast to you, I wouldn't rise.

A man's mistakes (if I may lecture you), his worst acts,
aren't out of character, as he'd like to think,
are not put on him by power or stress or too much to drink,

but are simply a worse self he consents to be. Thus
there is no mistaking you. I marvel that there's
so much disrespect for a man just being himself, being his errors.

'I never met a worse man than myself,'
Thoreau said. When we're our best selves, we can all
afford to say that. Self-respect is best when marginal.

And when the office of the presidency will again
accommodate that remark, it may be held by better men
than you or me. Meantime, I hear there is music in your house,

your women wear queens' wear, though winds howl outside,
and I say, that's all right, the man should have some ease,
but does anyone say to your face who you really are?

No, they say *Mr. President,* while any young person
feels free to call me *voter, believer,* even *causer.*
And if I were also a pray-er, a man given to praying,

(I'm often in fact careless about great things, like you)
and I wanted to pray for your office, as in fact I do,
the words that would come to me would more likely be

god change you than *god bless the presidency.*
I would pray, *God cause the President to change.*
As I myself have been changed, first my head, then my heart,

so that I no longer pretend that I don't swindle or kill
when there is swindling and killing on my nation's part.
Well. Go out into your upstairs hall tonight with this letter.

Generous ghosts must walk that house at night,
carrying draughts of the Republic like cold water
to a man parched after too much talk and wine and smoke.

Hear them. They are elected ghosts, though some will be radicals
and all may want to tell you things you will not like.
It will seem dark in the carpeted hall, despite the nightlights

in the dull sconces. Make the guard let you pass.
'If you are the President,' a shade with a water glass
will ask you (and this is all I ask), calling you by name,

himself perhaps a famous name, 'If you are the President,
and things in the land have come to all this shame,
why don't you try doing something new? This building rose,

laborious as a dream, to house one character:
man trusting man anew. That's who each tenant is
—or an impostor, as some of us have been.'

1969

Accidents of Birth

Je vois les effroyables espaces de l'Univers qui m'enferment, et je me trouve attaché à un coin de cette vaste étendue, sans savoir pourquoi je suis plutôt en ce lieu qu'en un autre, ni pourquoi ce peu de temps qui m'est donné à vivre m'est assigné à ce point plutôt qu'à un autre de toute l'éternité qui m'a précédé, et de toute qui me suit.

—Pascal, *Pensées sur la religion*

The approach of a man's life out of the past is history, and the approach of time out of the future is mystery. Their meeting is the present, and it is consciousness, the only time life is alive. The endless wonder of this meeting is what causes the mind, in its inward liberty of a frozen morning, to turn back and question and remember. The world is full of places. Why is it that I am here?

—Wendell Berry, *The Long-Legged House*

Spared by a car or airplane crash or
cured of malignancy, people look
around with new eyes at a newly
praiseworthy world, blinking eyes like these.

For I've been brought back again from the
fine silt, the mud where our atoms lie
down for long naps. And I've also been
pardoned miraculously for years
by the lava of chance which runs down
the world's gullies, silting us back.
Here I am, brought back, set up, not yet
happened away.

But it's not this random
life only, throwing its sensual
astonishments upside down on
the bloody membranes behind my eyeballs,
not just me being here again, old
needer, looking for someone to need,
but you, up from the clay yourself,
as luck would have it, and inching
over the same little segment of earth-
ball, in the same little eon, to

meet in a room, alive in our skins,
and the whole galaxy gaping there
and the centuries whining like gnats—
you, to teach me to see it, to see
it with you, and to offer somebody
uncomprehending, impudent thanks.

At the Confluence of the Colorado and the Little Colorado

For Stewart and Lee Udall

Where the two rivers come together—one cold,
one desert-warm—the party beached the raft to swim.
A blue aileron, looking new, lay on the bank
and Dennis put his shirt and bluejeans in it,
out of the wind that had blown his hat away.
Across the canyon, silver in the sun,
the fuselage glinted. The wreck was ten years old,
two liners that had come together in broad day,
dropping their metal feathers,
and two tribes of travelers who settled then
where the wind told them to settle.

To that lost Indian tribe, who farmed this dry grandeur once,
they might have seemed to be surrogates of gods
(anything but gods, these downcast mortals,
anything but wrathful, they fell bemused
at various unfulfillments, at sheer bad luck)
as they descended, shorn of all human gear
and taking what they found: the shimmering desert air,
white water, the hot shale.
                                                  And the hectoring solitude
that now made the rafters douse and romp and chatter,
a solitude that reverts to the subject of death
whenever the conversation of live things lags.

Poem

The swans on the river, a great
flotilla in the afternoon sun
in October again.

In a fantasy, Yeats saw himself appear
to Maud Gonne as a swan,
his plumage fanning his desire.

One October at Coole Park
he counted fifty-nine wild swans.
He flushed them into a legend.

Lover by lover is how he said they flew,
but one of them must have been without a mate.
Why did he not observe that?

We talk about Zeus and Leda and Yeats
as if they were real people, we identify constellations
as if they were drawn there on the night.

Cygnus and Castor & Pollux
are only ways of looking at
scatterings of starry matter,

a god putting on swan-flesh
to enter a mortal girl
is only a way of looking at love-trouble.

The violence and calm of these big fowl!
When I am not with you
I am always the fifty-ninth.

The Seasons' Difference

Here on the warm strand, where a turquoise light
without horizon combs and breaks, menacing
only as love or morning menace
the man-made errors of the world,
I receive a contrary vision:
For an instant I seem to stand alone
under a lead sky, in late afternoon,
in winter. The gray will thicken soon
to snow, and I desire this vision
as one desires his own smell and person.
The mind waiting for snow is the true mind.
Numb tongue and lips speak for it clumsily
but turquoise baubles cannot distract it for long.

Before the thick-lipped winter-thinker
in me can explain, you explain. *Both,*
you call from where the sheer ocean
shelves off from a man's height, *Both,*
with the impatience of summer
and whatever is always between us.
As if to show me how to take a season
on its own terms, you ride a glass sea-slide
into the foamy shallows where I stand,
gray and stubborn as a snowman.

For Two Lovers in the Year 2075 in the Canadian Woods

If you have lips and forests,
you creatures years from now,
here are some lines to tell you
that we were among your trees
in extraordinary flesh
and ecstasy now gone,
and our tongues looked for each other
and after that for words.

If you have August moonrise
and bodies to undress,
here are some words we've left you
when we had had our say.
Put them beside your cummings,
if you still carry books,
not as sweet as Landor,
not as quick as Donne,
wrap them in still-warm clothing
beside your sleeping bag
for when you want to speak.

These trees are stirred by ghosting,
not only ours but others'.
Enjoy the feathery presences,
no sadder than your own,
they gather from the past—
last August's moan and whisper,
the leaves renew the weavings
and lacings of the flesh.
Here is the sound of ours.

Memoirs

For Richard and Charlee Wilbur

Even when he was a child, the Emperor
remembered, cartography had been a passion.
He had vexed his mother by turning carpets over
and drawing on the undersides in chalk
the map of Europe from memory or after his own heart.
Mountains and their defiles, rivers and plains,
rather than kingdoms, were what he said he drew.

The Empress-Mother, small by now and round,
her feet resting comfortably on the Aubusson
at Saint Cloud, said rather irritably, Maps?
Maps? We were much too poor in Corsica to have rugs.

Give and Take

(Christmas, after a death in the family)

What are these presents   Look how many
have come unwrapped   & the stockings
tight with tangerines & kisses
& heavy Swiss things   deserved &
undeserved & deserved again
before you can open them   Look
they are stolen by little unwrappers
who whisper at dawn   who
come downstairs in their bedclothes
to loot & grow older & us

Presence of love in this house
gifts of it   words of it
words for giving assent   about taking too
taking too much   Tell the children not to
Why not   tell ourselves not to
it is more blessed not to   but we take
naturally   we take to one another
wrapped in flesh tinsel & tissue   we are all
gaudy rejoicers in taking   two's   those two
we two   some alone   some alone

It's about time   & about love   both
this impatience to unwrap   to wrap
arms around airy expensive unholdable
things   Swiss chocolate kisses & pine
trees or spruce   one another
Often we're shiny & wanted
Tinsel is cheap   We believe it
It wouldn't glisten without eyes

No one in the whole world was ever bad
we lie   greedy or not   Hurry up   unwrap
this love is for you   where's mine
Hug the world now & thank it

Because over it hangs like our green wreath
a black wreath   a prescience
of days coming to some end
Not all spruce-smell & singing is gay
Some are not here

Boxes gape open   compartments of time
Is it nicely snowing outside this snug room
or do we stand suddenly in an autumn field
Who is the one in the box   Will God unwrap her
gladly & tell her the rest
after we've tied her up grassily
& told her goodnight   Lie still now
we've told her   God will be glad
at what we've thought of to bring him
He who has everything   sooner or later

It's hard giving people   Lucky is our habit
Are we lucky   still clutching here   losing
& trying to give back to the Indian giver
while the dark wreath reminds on the door
Just now in the early twilight
how dark the hemlock wreath
already unchristmassed
& these are not mechanical Swiss things
we are asked to rewrap & return
We do it as well as we can
but we're small thieves by nature   & keepers

In the autumn field where we left her
stands a distant insatiable relative
waiting to take what is his   to ease us
or torture us   which   into a box
where we'll lie still   still murmuring
give me   love me   smaller & smaller
asking in a voice of tiny unwrapping
astonishment   *mine   is it really for me*

Parents

For Vanessa Meredith and Samuel Wolf Gezari

What it must be like to be an angel
or a squirrel, we can imagine sooner.

The last time we go to bed good,
they are there, lying about darkness.

They dandle us once too often,
these friends who become our enemies.

Suddenly one day, their juniors
are as old as we yearn to be.

They get wrinkles where it is better
smooth, odd coughs, and smells.

It is grotesque how they go on
loving us, we go on loving them.

The effrontery, barely imaginable,
of having caused us. And of how.

Their lives: surely
we can do better than that.

This goes on for a long time. Everything
they do is wrong, and the worst thing,

they all do it, is to die,
taking with them the last explanation,

how we came out of the wet sea
or wherever they got us from,

taking the last link
of that chain with them.

Father, mother, we cry, wrinkling,
to our uncomprehending children and grandchildren.

My Mother's Life

A woman neither young nor old, she moves
along the dark suburban street
swaddled against the night and cold
in a bright cloak. Only her face
and her small ankles are exposed
as she walks briskly toward some life she walks toward.
She is tired, and I think at this moment
she is expecting nothing. Not this. *Not this:*

a klieg light spots her from the sky
across the street. Out of the air it asks.
It asks something of the face she turns upward
to the supernatural light. I don't hear the question,
the illumination dazes the other senses.
And in the dream I watch the woman's face
as composure and surprise dispute its plainness.

I think she gives the right answer, before
the light dims, bluing, then purpling the retina.

Ideogram

For William and Emmy Maxwell

I am trying to describe to you a river at first light.
The water is glassy, under a scud of mist.
It is taking the color of the new sky
but the mist has something else in mind than pink—
a force of discoloration, it would have everything white.
On the far bank are serried low hills, tree clusters,
occasionally the lights of a car.

This river I want you to see is being remembered.
I tell you this not to make us self-conscious
or conscious of words, but hoping to heighten
the peculiar vividness of a thing imagined.
I put no waterbird or craft on the surface:
the poem is absolutely quiet at about 5 a.m.
Rose-gray water slips away to left and right, silky,
upstream and downstream, just before sunrise,
just before we are called away,
you who don't know me, I who don't know you.

Soon it will be full light. We will blink this river away
and my talking to you, a stranger, as if I knew you,
as if our partaking a strange river at the edge of light
had been no impertinence—this will yield to another subject.
A river talked away may be the new subject, or,
Mist burned off by the sun, an ancient, common figure,
a nearly dead metaphor, for enlightenment, and
it occurs to me now that someone may have already
accomplished this for you, hundreds of years ago,
someone deft with a brush, in China.

Grievances

Now and perpetually, over
the dark side of the earth
flows a tide of wakefulness
through chosen men and women,
the changing hostels of grievance,
which travels by night.

In Dublin a huge old man
is falling to sleep, having for hours
rehearsed words for tomorrow
to say to his shiftless nephew,
his sister's son, who's been making
the flat upstairs a brothel

while a tossing girl in Rio
abruptly turns on the light
and getting out of bed
puts on a flannel bathrobe
and goes to the typewriter.
I have forgiven you for the last time . . .

This is the after-edge of night.
Seen from far off, it's the last
dark segment before the purple band
that glows at the edge of the ball,
the edge of the planet that is
spinning again into sunlight.

Not thirty degrees east
the surly hosts are throwing off
the fit, or trying to, faced
with sun-cheer and bird-cheer,
the mindless smiles of dogs and children,
accumulating evidence of day.

Meanwhile and perpetually, these
hoboes make a sour clock of our globe.

Choosing you once or often,
or settling in, they pass
through your town each night
and have to have lodging.

For the life of me, I can't
turn one away. In the morning
they write on the fence by the door
in ciphers no man can erase:
this one mails the letters
or, *this one says the words.*

Here and There

For Sylvia Shelly

Whose spirit is this? we said, because we knew
It was the spirit that we sought and knew
That we should ask this often as she sang.

—Wallace Stevens, "The Idea of Order at Key West"

I

Here in the north, a cold gray morning
does not deter the still-mating birds:
two orioles, a wood thrush? I'm not good
at this quick argot, so particular
but sounding all alike to a foreigner.
There's no heat in the house of course in May
unless I light a fire. Stevens
I think would have lighted one today
and, comfortable with my betters, I do too.

II

There in Key West, the singer lies asleep,
perhaps under a fan, after playing late
at the café. They kept her playing and singing
by the edge of the warm gulf
(after she'd watched the sun drop into it,
staying to cup Hesperus in her small hands
against the wind that rises suddenly then,
until his flame caught)—they wouldn't let her stop
at one o'clock. Now the current
runs past the island very fast
as if in panic. But the trees flower
calmly in the heat outside her house.

III

Now there are whole mindfuls of climate
in Connecticut and Florida, ideas
of moisture and drought, cold and hot—
living and dead, for that matter.
Think of how many ideas are dancing in pairs.

The idea of Wallace Stevens dancing alone
is picked up and held in mind briefly,
here and there, like a birdcall. What
is the difference between ourselves and ghosts?
Only that we move awkwardly through the air.

IV

While my cold birds chirrup—I dare not say mindlessly—
in Connecticut, and the crackling on the hearth
begins to warm me, I hear as well
the tart music of last night in the piano bar
glassed in from the green-lighted water off Key West,
the laughter struck with certain resonances
that is Sylvia's particular call,
though I think she is still asleep,
perhaps with a ceiling fan turning slowly
above her bed, between two ideas, a gulf and an ocean.

Remembering Robert Lowell

The message you brought back again and again
from the dark brink had the glitter of truth.
From the beginning, you told it as memoir:
even though you didn't cause it,
the memoirs said of the trouble they recounted,
it was always your familiar when it came.

Your language moved slowly toward our language
until we saw that we were all immigrants—
had perhaps been shipped as convicts—
from the land of your reluctant indictment,
a land of our consent, if not of our doing.

It was your jokes and stories, when you were alive,
the wry imitations and the bad boy's laugh,
that roped us from the brink you led us to.
We will miss that laughter, left to the glittering poems,
the raw gist of things.

To punish the bearer of evil tidings
it is our custom to ask his blessing.
This you gave. It dawns on each of us separately now
what this entails.

Dreams of Suicide

In sorrowful memory of Ernest Hemingway, Sylvia Plath, and John Berryman

I

I reach for the awkward shotgun not to disarm
you, but to feel the metal horn,
furred with the downy membrane of dream.
More surely than the unicorn,
you are the mythical beast.

II

Or I am sniffing an oven. On all fours
I am imitating a totemic animal
but she is not my totem or the totem
of my people, this is not my magic oven.

III

If I hold you tight by the ankles,
still you fly upward from the iron railing.
Your father made these wings,
after he made his own, and now from beyond
he tells you *fly down*, in the voice
my own father might say *walk, boy*.

In Loving Memory of the Late Author of *Dream Songs*

Friends making off ahead of time
on their own, I call that willful, John,
but that's not judgment, only argument
such as we've had before.
I watch a shaky man climb
a cast-iron railing in my head, on
a Mississippi bluff, though I had meant
to dissuade him. I call out, and he doesn't hear.

'Fantastic! Fantastic! Thank thee, dear Lord'
is what you said we were to write on your stone,
but you go down without so much as a note.
Did you wave jauntily, like the German ace
in a silent film, to a passerby, as the paper said?
We have to understand how you got
from here to there, a hundred feet straight down.
Though you had told us and told us,
and how it would be underground
and how it would be for us left here,
who could have plotted that swift chute
from the late height of your prizes?
For all your indignation, your voice
was part howl only, part of it was caress.
Adorable was a word you threw around,
fastidious John of the gross disguises,
and *despair* was another: 'this work of almost despair.'

Morale is what I think about all the time
now, what hopeful men and women can say and do.
But having to speak for you, I can't
lie. 'Let his giant faults appear, as sent
together with his virtues down,' the song says.
It says suicide is a crime
and that wives and children deserve better than this.
None of us deserved, of course, you.

Do we wave back now, or what do we do?
You were never reluctant to instruct.
I do what's in character, I look for things
to praise on the riverbanks and I praise them.
We are all relicts, of some great joy, wearing black,
but this book is full of marvelous songs.
Don't let us contract your dread recidivism
and start falling from our own iron railings.
Wave from the fat book again, make us wave back.

John and Anne

> I would call the subject of Anne Frank's *Diary* even more mysterious than St. Augustine's, and describe it as: the conversion of a child into a person. . . . It took place under very special circumstances which—let us now conclude as she concluded—though superficially unfavorable, were in fact highly favorable to it; she was *forced* to mature, in order to survive; the hardest challenge, let's say, that a person can face without defeat is the best for him.
>
> —John Berryman, "The Development of Anne Frank"

Are you grown up now, John, now that it's over?
Do you sit around sober and peaceful these days,
listening to the big people's palaver,
nobody interrupting, nobody famished for praise?

(We have to fable some such place of good talk
—*Nobody listens to me,* the child would shout—
because we ourselves remain shrill little folk:
there must be somewhere we'll hear each other out.)

Do you engage your friends in the ghostly scene
with decorum you could only parody as a man:
Anne Bradstreet and the Governor, St. Augustine,
Jarrell, and this other, child-woman Anne?

It was a long time coming, this quiet,
this hard adulthood, after tantrums of enquiry.
Nobody answers my questions, the child would shout.
You went from the one bottle to the other, thirsty.

'The hardest challenge, let's say, that a person can face
without defeat is the best for him.' She could weep
at Auschwitz for the naked gypsy girls gassed in that place.
Dying at Belsen, she helped you to grow up.

Dying Away

Homage to Sigmund Freud

'Toward the person who has died
we adopt a special attitude:
something like admiration
for someone who has accomplished
a very difficult task,' he said,

and now hospitals and rest homes
are filled with heroes and heroines
in smocks, at their outsized, unwonted tasks,
now the second date on tombstones is a saint's day
and there is no craven in any graveyard,

no malingerer there, no trivial person.
It is you and I, still milling around,
who evade our callings, incestuous
in our love for the enduring trees and the snowfall,
for brook-noise and coins, songs, appetites.

And with the one we love most,
the mated one we lose track of ourselves in—
who's giving, who's taking that fleshy pleasure?—
we call those calmings-away, those ecstasies
dyings, we see them as diligent rehearsals.

The love of living disturbs me,
I am wracked like a puritan by eros and health,
almost undone by brotherhood, rages
of happiness seize me, the world, the fair world,
and I call on the name of the dark healer, Freud.

His appetites, songs, orgasms died away,
his young brother, his daughter, his huge father,
until he saw that the aim of life was death.
But a man cannot learn heroism from another,
he owes the world some death of his own invention.

Then he said, 'My dear Schur, you certainly remember
our first talk. You promised me then not to forsake me
when my time came. Now it is nothing but torture
and makes no sense any more.'
Schur gave him centigrams of morphine.

At what cost he said it, so diligent of life,
so curious, we can't guess
who are still his conjurings. He told us
it is impossible to imagine our own deaths,
he told us, this may be the secret of heroism.

The Revenant

> Kilgore Trout owned a parakeet named Bill. . . . Trout sneered and muttered to his parakeet about the end of the world.
>
> "Any time now," he would say. "And high time, too."
>
> It was Trout's theory that the atmosphere would become unbreathable soon.
>
> Trout supposed that when the atmosphere became poisonous, Bill would keel over a few minutes before Trout did. He would kid Bill about that. "How's the old respiration, Bill?" he'd say, or, "Seems like you've got a touch of the old emphysema, Bill," or, "We never discussed what kind of a funeral you want, Bill. You never even told me what your religion is." And so on.
>
> He told Bill that humanity deserved to die horribly, since it had behaved so cruelly and wastefully on a planet so sweet. "We're all Heliogabalus, Bill," he would say. This was the name of a Roman emperor who had a sculptor make a hollow, life-size iron bull with a door on it. The door could be locked from the outside. The bull's mouth was open. That was the only other opening to the outside.
>
> Heliogabalus would have a human being put into the bull through the door, and the door would be locked. And sounds the human being made in there would have to come out of the mouth of the bull. Heliogabalus would have guests in for a nice party, with plenty of food and wine and beautiful women and pretty boys—and Heliogabalus would have a servant light kindling. The kindling was under dry firewood—which was under the bull.
>
> —Kurt Vonnegut, *Breakfast of Champions*

I am a spirit now. After that death,
I died in great pain only once, a cancer
in my stomach the size of a melon,
and with morphine I could keep silence.
Sometimes when the grandchildren shouted at play
outside the house, I felt the passion to shout too,
but remembered the lesson.

When they put me inside the clanking belly
I understood what I had to do, I had
simply to keep quiet. As it grew hot

I thrashed my arms and legs as quietly as I could,
the way a deaf-mute might scream. The noise
of the fire was enough to keep him from hearing
my scrabbling, and I was careful.
Denied the expression of screams, my body
danced out its message. In my mind
I could see the jowly emperor's pain.
'Last time, it bellowed as if in orgasm,'
he shouted to the disappointed guests,
some of them already lost in drink or love-making.

I gained two stages of progress by that dance
but Heliogabalus did not profit from my show
of continence, could not learn anything
from his iron beast, speaking a blessed silence.
He was not elevated by that existence.

Crossing Over

> It was now early spring, and the river was swollen and turbulent; great cakes of floating ice were swinging heavily to and fro in the turbid waters. Owing to a peculiar form of the shore, on the Kentucky side, the land bending far out into the water, the ice had been lodged and detained in great quantities, and the narrow channel which swept round the bend was full of ice, piled one cake over another, thus forming a temporary barrier to the descending ice, which lodged, and formed a great undulating raft. . . . Eliza stood, for a moment, contemplating this unfavorable aspect of things.
>
> —Harriet Beecher Stowe, *Uncle Tom's Cabin* (Chapter VII, "The Mother's Struggle")

That's what love is like. The whole river
is melting. We skim along in great peril,

having to move faster than ice goes under
and still find foothold in the soft floe.

We are one another's floe. Each displaces the weight
of his own need. I am fat as a bloodhound,

hold me up. I won't hurt you. Though I bay,
I would swim with you on my back until the cold

seeped into my heart. We are committed, we
are going across this river willy-nilly.

No one, black or white, is free in Kentucky,
old gravity owns everybody. We're weighty.

I contemplate this unfavorable aspect of things.
Where is something solid? Only you and me.

Has anyone ever been to Ohio?
Do the people there stand firmly on icebergs?

Here all we have is love, a great undulating
raft, melting steadily. We go out on it

anyhow. I love you, I love this fool's walk.
The thing we have to learn is how to walk light.

Not Both

> . . . I sleep on. And again
> Old Zack, pore ole white-trash—croker sack dragging—
> Is out to scrounge coal off the L & N tracks.
> Old Mag at it too, face knobby, eyes bleared,
> Mouth dribbling with snuff, skirts swinging
> Above the old brogan she's fixed for her clubfoot,
> And dragging her own sack for coal.
> They don't hear the whistle. Or Zack's
> Just stubborn, born democrat, knowing damned well
> That the coal, it is his, and by rights.
> Then the whistle again, in outrage and anguish.
>
> And now I wake up, or not. If I don't
> It blows on like hell, brakes screaming,
> And Mag, of a sudden, is down. The brogan she wears
> For the clubfoot, it looks like it's caught
> In a switch-V—the coal chute starts here.
> And I stand in a weedy ditch, my butterfly
> Net in my hand, my chloroform jar,
> Mount box, and canteen strung on me—and Zack,
> He keeps pulling. She's up. Zack bends at the brogan.
> The whistle goes wild. Brakes scream. I stare.
>
> Zack's up, foot's out! Or is it? A second she's standing,
> Then down—now over both rails—
> Down for good, and the last
> Thing I see is his hands out. To grab her, I reckoned.
>
> —Robert Penn Warren, "Recollection in Upper Ontario"

The club-footed woman was mangled by the train.
Her husband was trying to free her foot from the switch-V
or he was holding her foot there so the train would kill her.

The tall girl and her over-handsome brother
who lived those years together in the city
while she practiced harpsichord and he the law,
till one day he married a rich woman, and she,
months later, an older man, a lawyer—
they were lovers those seven years, or they weren't.

The woman who sailed her dinghy out in the Bay
in the fall blow—autumn is for beginnings—

and was found miles from the zigzagging sailboat
that she knew like a husband—either she sought
a way to drown or the Chesapeake taught her, not both.

Either before I die I'll falter and tell
the strange secret I was given once as a token
or I'll manage to carry it with me.

Somebody knows or nobody knows these answers.

One of those two appalling things is true too.

REM Sleep

> The first indication that sleep might be more than a unitary state occurred when several researchers, Nathaniel Klietman, Eugene Aserinsky, and William Dement, noted the occurrence of rapid eye movements at various intervals during a night's sleep. As a result of these findings, sleep was divided into two major categories: rapid-eye-movement, REM sleep, and an independent stage of nonrapid-eye-movement or NREM sleep. . . . Considerable interest has focused on REM sleep since it was noted that dream recall frequently followed awakening from this sleep phase.
>
> —*McGraw-Hill Encyclopedia of Science & Technology*

> I direct that my body not be buried until such time as it shows signs of decomposition. I mention this because during my illness there have already been moments of deathly numbness when my heart and pulse stopped beating.
>
> —N. V. Gogol, Last Will and Testament

> "They've stolen my linen from under my frock coat.
> There's a draft through a crack. But there's no way to get through it.
>
> Even Christ suffered less
> before waking up in the grave!"
> The subterranean cry did not shake the depths.
> Two men had a drink on the grave.
> We enjoy funerals just as
> you enjoy hearing how Gogol was buried.
>
> Unseal his coffin freezing in the snow.
> Gogol, writhing, lies on his side.
> His twisted toenail has torn the lining in his boot.
>
> —Andrei Voznesensky, translated by Vera Dunham and F. W. Tjalsma, "The Interment of Nicolai Vasilich Gogol"

What are the two poor children thinking there,
thrashing nightly behind my lids,
trapped behind the soft eyelids like little Gogols?

'Do not bury us,' they spell out every day
in colored crayons, 'until you're sure we're dead,
until our orbs show signs of discoloration.'

Can they communicate there, the two inseparables?

Or at that distance apart does the flesh muffle sound,
the tamped cells stifle their cries like rained-on soil?

And what kind of instinct do you call the blind health
that bids them forget, every blessed morning,
the terrible entombment?

Sometimes I hear one eye say to another
in singsong, making an old-country joke of it,
'What an unlucky dream I dreamt last night. If I
believed in dreams. . . .'

Of Kindness

For Harriet Skidmore Arnold

> And the behavior released in us, by such confrontations, is, essentially, a surprised affection. . . . Maybe altruism is our most primitive attribute.
>
> —Lewis Thomas, *The Medusa and the Snail*

Where people live on earth there is a kind
of water table, a reservoir that rises and falls,
man-made, mysterious, our chemistry and purpose.
The fluid it holds is sweet to us,
we've caught it over and over
the way the thirsty ocean catches the rain.
This is the tribe's own drink. It flows
over populated land like history. It stands
in cisterns, rare as fortunate history.

There's never quite enough to slake us all.
We come to the wellhead daily and thirsty.
Daily and thirsty we're given the chance to drink
and to draw water—to carry some, uphill,
in leather buckets, on a pole across our shoulders
or on the flanks of burros, in the hot sun,
where dust is the general rule. We carry it,
and at the wellhead we wolf some down.

Does this wetness buoy us, like the bucket
of water that's all it takes to float a warship?
Like the cup of blood that's called grace?
At the fountain of Aesculapius (I've heard this story)
halfway up a mountain in the Aegean,
an unthinking traveler washed his sweat away
in the spring's sweet marble trough,
so that the little accidental tribe
he had climbed with knew angry drought;
while elsewhere at that moment,
attentive on the desert of her dying,
an old Spanish woman drew,
from a secret rivulet she knew,

laughter that doused her folk with crystal
that they could drink and go across without her.

Birds and the nearer animals are always
chiding us to be attentive to this flux. Swallows
riffling the surface of a pond
are cousins and reminders of our kind.

This is most of what is known about kindness
among our dry kind.

Examples of Created Systems

For Robert Penn Warren and Eleanor Clark

I. the stars

We look out at them on clear nights, thrilled
rather than comforted—brilliance and
distance put us in mind of our
own burnings and losses. And then who
flung them there, in a sowing motion
suggesting that random is beautiful?

II. archipelagoes

Or again, the islands that the old
cartographers, triangulating
their first glimpses of bays and peaks, set
down, and which the rich traveler, from
a high winter chair, chooses among
today—chains of jade thrown across the
torso of the sea-mother, herself
casually composed.

III. work camps and prisons

The homeless
Solzhenitsyn, looking at Russia,
saw a configuration of camps
spotting his homeland, 'ports' where men
and women were forced to act out
the birth-throes of volcanic islands,
the coral patience of reefs, before
a 'ship,' a prison train, bore them down
that terrible archipelago
conceived and made by men like ourselves.

IV. those we love

Incorrigibly (it is our nature)
when we look at a map we look for
the towns and valleys and waterways
where loved people constellate, some of

them from our blood, some from our own loins.
This fair scattering of matter is
all we will know of creation, at
first hand. We flung it there, in a learned
gesture of sowing—random, lovely.

From *Partial Accounts: New and Selected Poems* (1987)

The American Living Room: A Tract

For Michael, Katherine, Robert, and David

I

Ideally, you should be in your own
when you read this. Think of it as an oddity—
the one indoor space where living
is deliberately pursued, as in others
we transact dining, sleeping, bathing,
perhaps TV or children. Wherever there are two,
one should be kitchen. For the rich,
rooms can be spun out indefinitely:
drawing-, dressing-, morning-, and special
chambers called library, pantry, nursery.
Many still house their cars.

II

Most people inhabit shelters too small
to partition off with words, and always
some people have none. Is it better
to feel at fault for this, or not
to feel at fault? The meagerest American house
is a gross Hilton compared to where most people
take shelter on the inclement world.
To start with, feel fortunate.

III

You have made the effort to dress yourself
in character, probably well beyond the requirement
of mere covering—you have already risked
that much misunderstanding. Then comes
this second habiliment, no matter how
reluctant or minimal a statement,
a room which gives you away: with the things
you've acquired at cost, the things you've been given
and kept, the things you choose to exhibit.
The accumulation seems to have been only partly voluntary.
Yet no one you'd want to know could stay

for a month, in a rented room in Asia, without
this telltale silt beginning to settle.
When people die, their children have to come dig
for them like Winckelmanns, among many false Troys.

IV

Prisons recognize the need to arrest
this form of identity. Cells
are deliberately ill-fitted uniforms
which you are issued to wear over
the deliberately ill-fitted cloth ones. You
are put there to forgo living.

Military quarters may appear more permissive,
yet the space for personal effects is limited
and subject to unscheduled inspection. Nobody
is encouraged to bring along a two-volume dictionary,
a Hopi mask, a valuable paperweight, to a war
or to the interminable rehearsals of camp and shipboard.

V

The room we're in now is like something you've said,
whether offhand or considered. It's in a dialect
that marks you for a twentieth-century person
(enthusiastic about this? dragging your feet?),
rich or poor or—more commonly—a little of both;
belonging to a nation and an eclectic culture.
The room risks absurdity, as you risked that again
when you put your clothes on this morning,
but because it is capable of being judged
apart from you, in your absence, the risk is greater.
Why has he got and kept this, and only this?
anyone can ask. *Why so much?* To others
this room is what your scent is to a dog.
You can't know it or help it.

VI

With us in America, a person who has a printed poem
is likely to have a living room (though not always—

there will always be some to whom poetry is not an amenity).
For reasons of its own, poetry has come to this,
with us. It has somehow gone along
with the privileges of the nation
it intends to change, to dispossess of material demons.
Admittedly, this is part of its present difficulty.

For the moment, though, you are holding this poem.
Its aim is that of any artifact: to ingratiate.
It would like nothing better
than to be added to the dear clutter here.

The Jain Bird Hospital in Delhi

Outside the hotel window, unenlightened pigeons
weave and dive like Stukas on their prey,
apparently some tiny insect brother.
(In India, the attainment of nonviolence
is considered a proper goal for human beings.)
If one of the pigeons should fly into the illusion

of my window and survive (the body is no illusion
when it's hurt) he could be taken across town to the bird
hospital where Jains, skilled medical men,
repair the feathery sick and broken victims.
There, in reproof of violence
and of nothing else, live Mahavira's brothers and sisters.

To this small, gentle order of monks and nuns
it is bright Vishnu and dark Shiva who are illusion.
They trust in faith, cognition, and nonviolence
to release them from rebirth. They think that birds
and animals—like us, some predators, some prey—
should be ministered to no less than men and women.

The Jains who deal with creatures (and with laymen)
wear white, while their more enterprising hermit brothers
walk naked and are called *the sky-clad.* Jains pray
to no deity, human kindness being their sole illusion.
Mahavira and those twenty-three other airy creatures
who turned to saints with him, preached the doctrine of *ahimsa,*

which in our belligerent tongue becomes *nonviolence.*
It's not a doctrine congenial to snarers and poultrymen,
who every day bring to market maimed pheasants.
Numbers of these are brought in by the Jain brothers
and brought, to grow back wing-tips and illusions,
to one of the hospitals succoring such small quarry.

When strong and feathered again, the lucky victims
get reborn on Sunday mornings to the world's violence,

released from the roofs of these temples to illusion.
It is hard for a westerner to speak about men and women
like these, who call the birds of the air *brothers*.
We recall the embarrassed fanfare for Francis and his flock.

We're poor forked sky-clad things ourselves
and God knows prey to illusion—*e.g.*, I claim these brothers
and sisters in India, stemming a little violence, among birds.

The Three Sorts of Violence

For J. H. S.

I. natural

It is the test of us. It plumbs us
for a response until we have no answer
left to give but our names. It likes
to warp us. The test is to warp
to your own nature, like scrub growth
on sea cliffs or at the tree line
or in the long holding-out
against desert rack. Instinct
draws us to these handsome crooked things
who know nothing about flinching
or mythmaking, who have no choice
but to reply in character to ravage.

A lightning-fired oak will make
a broad oaken gesture for no one else
but itself before it falls in blue flame.
Understory trees, blind in the smother,
trust their cells to sign
their names once, blindfold, with a sure writhing.
Such signatures, flourished on the firestorm,
are no meek petition
but a will and testament.
Buried and far-blown seeds survive
who will probate it, laying fair claim
to leaf-shapes and leaf-dispositions—
lancelate or ovate, alternate or opposite—
and the distinctive head-shape of the grown tree.

And where violence effects mutation
among the species, this is to accommodate,
somehow, the long requirements
of brother raging-fire, of mother moving-water,
of sister-ice-who-stays-longer-than-winter.

Even with ourselves, where a family holds

to one place for a little while, gestures
recur from granddam to grandchild, and features
which violence can scribble something on
but not alter.

Perhaps we misuse
the word, about nature. Suppose
this is not violence that nature works
but something else, call it the stating
and then the restating of terms—
inexorable, arbitrary, playful,
and for any given one of us, beyond appeal.
But terms to be responded to in character.

No one ever promised us more.

II. man-made

Will I remember my own nature? instinct
asks, muttering to itself as it walks
the man-made surface of the earth.
To be caught off-guard is a fear
proper to a creature which has quit
its first habitat.

The tract itself is violent
where we go now—filled, pocked land
which we share with our unpredictable machinery.
We know the viciousness of machines
who misunderstand us, of laws
that get away from us or go mad.

Through our unnatural caution, or
through surprise, or in our dreams,
our devices try to change us.
And we are changed, if only in having
always to stop and ask—
when the car hurtles off on its own, when the tumor
takes possession: *will I remember my own nature?*

More and more the plants and animals
keep to themselves.

III. man-to-man

Here we lack models, and this is the violence
we respond to least surely. There is nothing
apparently we will not do to one another
or to the globe that was given us.

Homo hominem caedens, man killing man
is a new mutant. Among natural species
it would not survive. Among us it survives.

Nature is still strong in us.
Come, men and women, let us exterminate
this dangerous aberrant. He
is no brother of ours, nature exhorts us,

but perhaps we are too civilized for that.

Among Ourselves

Among ourselves like this, we are elaborate
not to slight the disastrous. Almost
superstitiously we tell
both accidental and malicious violences.
It is anecdotal and shivery—
planes, camps, cultures burn
in the pleasant room. One of us
may have known one of the bloodstained
or the charred. Most of us have children.
There is another round of drinks,
though we don't drink much anymore.
Nobody speaks
the wry assumption we leave off with:
at the worst, us as we find ourselves
here this evening, ironic dear survivors.

But after we disband, I think
the telling of lucky tales would be just
as observant as all this talking
of history personally. I have voted
and warred and wronged a good deal myself,
along with my forebears, most of it
well-meaning. Accountability
weighs on me, but so does happiness.
Why do we never recount that,
friends? And our lives,
what about them? Our sweet, deliberate lives?

In the Rif Mountains

(Northern Morocco)

Geology set this story down so long ago
it's a wonder it's still legible.
But the stylized hand is still clearly Arabic,
dark against the pale tan tablets of mountainside.

The violence of what's being told is belied
by the formal language of old rock,
as is the case with the later chronicles
written by, and about, smaller convulsions, men.
How shapely the various grammars that record
the brief cycles in which our substance roils and cools.
And the violence in each case is belied
a second time: the elegant calligraphy of rock and quill.

Yet close-to, the running, friable stone,
leached and pitted, no longer looks like writing
but like the spotted backs of old geology's hands.
They rest translucent, calm, the dreadful story told
and left here on these slanting tablets
for the tribes that will presently enter.

The tribes enter. They read the rocks as their Homer—
the source of a thousand years of manners,
the model for the hearts and seisms
that will harden into the Rifs of their dynasties
and then erode to build the foothills of their blood,
as it has been told.

Tree Marriage

In Chota Nagpur and Bengal
the betrothed are tied with threads to
mango trees, they marry the trees
as well as one another, and
the two trees marry each other.
Could we do that some time with oaks
or beeches? This gossamer we
hold each other with, this web
of love and habit is not enough.
In mistrust of heavier ties,
I would like tree-siblings for us,
standing together somewhere, two
trees married with us, lightly, their
fingers barely touching in sleep,
our threads invisible but holding.

Talking Back (To W. H. Auden)

for poetry makes nothing happen . . .

What it makes happen is small things,
sometimes, to some, in an area
already pretty well taken
care of by the senses. Thus, to
the eye, spruce needles fix the tufts
of new snow to the twigs so the
wind cannot dislodge them. They hold—
a metaphor. And in the ear,
the open, talking shapes, jet black,
in a snowbound brook, croon about
cold. And snow-foliage on the
high slopes dupes the eye, the whirring
spruces dupe the ear, and you think:
catkins, maybe, in February
or you think: whirring of doves' wings.
And ice underfoot is mica—
correspondences a man will
find, to his slight alteration,
always, where he pays attention—
on a walk after powder snow,
in a poem. As you well know.

Looked at carefully, nothing is sullen
but an inattentive creature.
Disorderly things praise order.
The exact details of our plight
in your poems, order revealed
by the closest looking, are things
I'm changed by and had never seen,
might never have seen, but for them.

Poetry makes such things happen
sometimes, as certain people do
at the right juncture of our lives.
Don't knock it, it has called across
the enchanted chasm of love

resemblances like rescue gear.
It is like finding on your tongue
right words to call across the floe
of arrogance to the wise dead,
of health to sickness, old to young.
Across this debt, we tell you so.

A Couple of Trees

The two oaks lean apart for light.
They aren't as strong as lone oaks
but in a wind they give each other lee.

Daily since I cleared them I can see
them, tempting to chain saw and ax—
two hardwoods, leaning like that for light.

A hurricane tore through the state one night,
picking up roof and hen-house, boat and dock.
Those two stood: leafless, twigless, giving lee.

Last summer ugly slugs unleafed the trees.
Environmental kids wrote *Gypsy Moths Suck.*
The V of naked oaks leaned to the light

for a few weeks, then put out slight
second leaves, scar tissue pale as bracts,
bandaged comrades, lending each other lee.

How perilous in one another's V
our lives are, yoked in this yoke:
two men, leaning apart for light,
but in a wind who give each other lee.

What I Remember the Writers Telling Me When I Was Young

For Muriel Rukeyser

Look hard at the world, they said—
generously, if you can
manage that, but hard. To see
the extraordinary data, you
have to distance yourself a
little, utterly. Learn the
right words for the umpteen kinds
of trouble that you'll see,
avoiding elevated
generics like *misery*,
wretchedness. And find yourself
a like spectrum of exact
terms for joy, some of them
archaic, but all useful.

Sometimes when they spoke to me I
could feel their own purposes
gathering. Language, the dark-
haired woman said once, is like
watercolor, it blots easily,
you've got to know what you're
after, and get it on quickly.
Everything gets watered
sooner or later with tears,
she said, your own or other
people's. The contrasts want to
run together and must not be
allowed to. They're what you
see with. Keep your word-hoard dry.

New Poems
(1958–83)

Of Possessions, in Winter

Scurvy with things, human brothers, human sisters,
I think we clutch our death of cold,
and it comes over me that the solstice
is made colder with fear of ourselves,
who are fearful god knows, and with lies about men and women,
who are good and bad certainly, but chiefly with the owning
of things which are not to be loved, not this way.

At the call of our prosperous conscience,
cold history has come back. It seems all
slave ships and massacres, though it was not,
being stippled and mysterious, like our own lives,
with grave occasional goodnesses. We should study those.
I am no slaver or killer, and though you have grievances
and though surely one instance of villainy is too many,
we are alive, we parley, where we dare to we love,
we say the truth. Summer is the change
we yearn the globe toward, meantime burning
what's comely but useless, for warmth—
things come from the sun, to burn.

It has turned spring before but never without love.
Perhaps the wobbling globe is seasonable
only with man's consent. We sit here
on the snowy plain in a circle of great stones,
an apparatus for inducing summer, set up
by long-dead elders. What we own is the leverage of the past
and now we must gather and take the fulcrum's stress.
If we are to make the sun come back
it will be by gifts and by divestment.

His Students

In the warm classroom, they give off heat.
It is winter, the lights are on, the pipes knock.
We are studying their youth. I talk.
I don't have a doctorate, but I know
The old way things were done and why.
Formerly I too was young. I sweat.
I've always believed in manners, and to this day
I will defend them. They are a small part of the truth.

I have become fond of this class. Dressed and coiffed
and intellectually equipped like so many Kaspar Hausers,*
they struggle into the Nürnberg of my Tuesdays,
taxing my powers of invention. Now they are asking
personal questions which do not bear
on youth, which have nothing to do with the subject,
youth. There's an atmosphere of guarded trust
in the room and I don't want to appear pedantic,
but after all, I am the instructor,
they sought me out. Or did I seek them out?
As they ask nosy, characteristic questions
I realize how interested I am in them
as young men and women, in their personal lives.
You can't study youth apart from the world
it has made, personally, out of the damnedest junk.
Nor are they as guileless as they pretend,
all raising their hands at once when I ask
who would like to explain age? Whoever I call on
will say something that sounds like his last respects.

I study them hard, but they will barely consent to leaf
through me, or their stereotype for me.
I wonder if I will ever be read again
after the present generation of teachers retires?

---

*Kaspar Hauser: 1812?–33, mysterious German foundling. He appeared in Nuremberg in 1828 in a state of semi-idiocy, and giving an incoherent account of his past, which he said he had spent in a dark prison hole.

So I read excerpts to them. I read a passage about an old war.
It is curiously lacking in violence (I shy
away from holocaust, just as they are obsessed with it),
but what I read is true and they are impressed.
How much better it sounds when I read it!
Perhaps it isn't really there on the page?
merely a trick of reading, a gift for explanation?

Meantime before the bell I remember to summarize.
(They won't do these things for themselves—
their notebooks are *graffiti,* though I still
ask that they be passed in at intervals.)
I summarize as impartially as I know how,
the essential differences, touched on this hour,
between youth and its opposite, age.

At the Prado

Carrying the guidebook you marked
how many years ago, I move,
comfortably foreign,
through the great museum,
for once knowing what I'm looking for.

Squiggles in the margins
record in ballpoint blue
only the things you liked
and I become graphologist
to the living, nervous hand
which only once breaks into words:
above where you underscored
Two admirable landscapes of his
are 'The Crossing of the Stygian Lake'
and 'Landscape with St. Jerome'
you've written, 'New to me—lovely blue.'

Charon, on the azure lake,
is ferrying a naked soul
(too small to be your soul)
from the gardens of bliss to torment.
Facing the dread shore,
the soul looks pale, but composed.
In the other picture,
a gentle lion is purring
in Jerome's little cell
while in a field nearby
its uncouth brother bounds
to eat an astonished peasant.
Over both the scenes
(though sullied in the first
by the resinous smoke of hell)
the color of impartiality
floats, an emblem new to me.
Alive, you walked both shores
of that lake, and both those lions fed,

but now it is Patinir's blue,
ambiguous welkin you call my attention to.

Journal Entry (With the Udalls, June 1968)

The moon came up late, because the sandstone bluff across the river rises perhaps 50 degrees from where I'd set my sleeping bag. First the cliff behind me took moonlight, then I sat up to watch the canyon wall running NE above us take color. The reds emerged in the light of the full moon, the way I have occasionally seen autumn sumac and maple tell color by moonlight, or I suppose roses must do: I can't recall roses by moonlight though I must have seen them.

Finally toward the top of the bluff the glow became brighter and at last, only 30 or 40 feet below the top, the moon put out a bright edge, making the dark edge of the bluff dance on the retina. How many million times has this night of the planet's tilt occurred before there was a viewer from this crevice in the sand?

Later I woke and walked across the brilliant sand, past sleepers, to the edge of the bright rapids. Once there was a meteorite in the western notch where the Dipper was going away, lip-first. Then the moon was eaten by the opposite bluff, the one we slept under, having described a low southern arc, like the winter sun's. In the full moon, on my sleeping bag, I had been able to see to write with this pen a little tetrameter sonnet.

IN THE CANYON

Under the massive cliffs which the moon,
miser of color, gives color to,
on moon-colored sand at the end of June
hearing the rapids we've hurtled through,
seeing at the base of the talus strand
off the further shore, the whitewater crest
in the frenzy of running water stands,
and Scorpio follows the Dipper west.

The troubles of cities do not recede
from the mind. Rather, they nag like guilt,
as sometimes when I drink and feed,
in my delicate gluttony I've felt
the spectral hunger of Asia bite
my gut and whet my appetite.

Journal Entry (April 1969, Villa Serbelloni)

(I. Ferry Boats Dock at the Foot of the Steep Prospect Below His Window)

The celluloid boats scoot across the lake because (I think) someone puts chips of camphor at the stern. Surface tension keeps them afloat, or did ours in the bathtub in Darien.

(II. He Worries about His Credentials—Ought He to Be Writing Where Pliny the Younger Wrote?)

I am the revenant here. Walking on the castled promontory by a quarter moon, it is clear that the pines & beeches, the bells on the fishnets out in the lake, are the living tenants. (I thought they were cowbells—Longfellow apparently knew right off—see 'cadanabia.')

(III. His Luck)

What if I had stepped on the sunning lizard?
What if I had run over the child?

(IV. He Is Vain about 1. His Friendships 2. His Humility)

Among the guests, occasionally a great man, more than occasionally suggestions of great accomplishment. X knows that he is not, by this scale, a big man, and knows I am not one either. We talk late, each wishing that the other may presently, somehow, prove him wrong—a generous wish, born of liking.

(V. Between His Window and the Ferry Dock, Horse Chestnuts Do a Characteristic Thing)

Who told you to tie green Kleenex to all those fat sticks, *hippocastanzas?* What an intemperate green.

(VI. High Above the Villa, the Cowherds' Grass Fire Reminds Him of an Urban Grievance in Connecticut)

One alpine slope burns red and slow
Tonight, a displaced volcano.
It is a rite of spring, I guess—
Firing the old, they make new grass.

Across the Thames from me at home
Dow Chemical makes *Styrofoam*.
Electric glare napalms the black
Of night, the stars do not grow back.

(VII. A Poem from Charlotte's Note, 'A Short, Steep Walk to the Castle of Vezio')

'If Signor Attica suggests you descend to Varenna by the steep path in front of the castle, it would be wise not to follow the suggestion.'

(VIII. He Goes to Bed Early Again)

Where there are no parties or quarrels, there is seldom occasion to watch the sunrise.

April 1969 (Edited nostalgically in December for his friends)

A Vision of Good Secrets

If the kept secrets of our finished lives
Some day rise up, what a doomsday they will have:
From the numberless houses, deserts, caves
Of its human stay, each whole anatomy
Of the man's affection, and the woman's, each family
Of true deceptions, will be reunited, abler than old bones
To sing, and with more to sing about—a valley
Of buried secrets, rising to claim their own.

'Why were we secret?' one of the true may ask
Among the yawning bodies of affection
That wake on the valley floor. 'Why did I risk
My blood and hair and bones in that deception?'
Or another, more thoughtful secret ask, 'Hence-
forth how will a person relish hate or shame,
Or manage love without its reticence,
And everybody calling things by name?'

But then a voice will silence all who had slept
And the host of the false secrets will tremble
As the names are read of those that were well kept,
Of all with honest reason to dissemble.
All generous and well-intentioned lies,
All expensive silences, will earn eternal silence then,
But all vain secrets will that voice expose
Like the flaming souls of wicked medieval men.

Therefore, my secrets, shades of hate and fear
And love (who outnumbers all the tribes
As, when the names are published, will appear)
Prepare yourselves, so live that when that blast
Of bright exposure rends your flimsy robes
And you stand named and naked at the last,
One judging will say, after your long sleep,
This is my faithful secret, him I will keep.

The Quarrel

They went outside then, in the mild night,
Fumes of liquor and woodsmoke
Swathing the two men, a veil of mackerel cloud
Swathing the planet, the half-moon taking cloud
Like an old scow.
The wife kissed her husband's friend
And got into the car. Deliberately he spoke
Enough to make anger stir again
And they said goodnight.

In school once, he had had to find the flaw
In a scheme for perpetual motion:
Between two swinging magnets, at the full swing
A lead shield rose to cut the magnets' flow.
Such fields are not cut so.
This moon would cling
All night through the thickening shield of cloud,
And the tide answer from the ocean.
But their car drove off down the winding road
Centrifugal as a galaxy going away
And the words he had found to say
Swaddled him like a shroud.

'In the Middle of the Long Friendship'

In the middle of the long friendship, five
days of gentlest violence, love
building and brimming, what the hands
rifled by night, eyes by day would restore; rounds
of this, in the strange country where they met,
until parting at the shore, even the grief was sweet.

Poem to Me

Old marvel of will, me, famished for vanity
And ease, do you still rein in
And take account of general famine?
From what prowl do you slink home
Again, old slaverer, agrowl,
Remembering or dreaming of what duty?

And in this jungle of a world, what kin
Do you feel to those other weak
Beasts, sneaking and stealing,
Preferring a green flickering or a black night
To the general nourishment of the sun,
Whose only choice is choice of appetite?

Too proud to call, you howl softly, brother,
But always when you hunt
You nose out and leave some nourishment
For more than self or mate or spawn.
Not lion or horse, but not kite or vermin either,
I hear you howl to yourself
Over and over, so as not to forget, *Man. I am man.*

Housed (A Report on a Visiting Dog)

Your great horse of a dog has been sick
with a self-inflicted wound: he won't
stop licking a gash he incurred, a month ago,
just over the hill, in a real-life drama,
I think, a love triangle.
The veterinarian, a sleek, indoor Italian,
says this happens only to house pets—
a wild animal has better things to do.

My spirit too is idle and housed in March.
With books and cans of food in the walls,
I deceive myself that I neither stalk nor am stalked.
I sit up late in bed with a pencil and shirt cardboard.
The dog groans at the light, resettles.
Now I see a small welt has arisen, this poem.

English Accounts

I. Trelawny's Dream

Edward John Trelawny, who is imagined to speak the following lines in his late middle age, survived his friend Shelley by almost sixty years, and lies beside him in the Protestant Cemetery in Rome. He seems to have met no man or woman in a long life whom he could marvel at and love as he did Shelley. Trelawny had intended to convoy the poet and Edward Williams (and a cabin boy, Charles Vivian) when they sailed the *Ariel* out of Leghorn into the storm that drowned them, but Lord Byron's yacht, which he was commanding, was detained at the last minute by port authorities. He cremated the remains of his friends, and recovered the little boat, which appeared to have been run down by a larger vessel, though the violent squall into which the *Ariel* disappeared would have been enough to founder the keel-heavy boat which Trelawny himself had unwisely designed for the novice Shelley.

—W. M.

The dark illumination of a storm
and water-noise, chuckling along the hull
as the craft runs tight before it.
Sometimes Shelley's laughter wakes me here,
unafraid, as he was the day he dove
into water for the first time, a wooded pool
on the Arno, and lay like a conger eel
on the bottom—'where truth lies,' he said—
until I hauled him up.

But oftener the dream insists on all,
insists on retelling all.
                                        Ned Williams is the first
to see the peril of the squall. His shout
to lower sail scares the deck boy wide-eyed
and cuts off Shelley's watery merriment.
The big wind strokes the catboat like a kitten.
Riding the slate-gray hillocks, she is dragged
by the jib Ned Williams leaves to keep her head.
The kitten knows the wind is a madman's hand
and the bay a madman's lap.
As she scuds helpless, only the cockney boy

Charles Vivian and I, a dreamer and a child,
see the felucca loom abeam. Her wet lateen
ballooning in the squall, she cuts across
wind and seas in a wild tack, she is on us.
The beaked prow wrenches the little cabin
from the deck, tosses the poet slowly to the air—
he pockets his book, he waves to me and smiles—
then to his opposite element,
light going into darkness, gold into lead.
The felucca veers and passes, a glimpse of a face
sly with horror on her deck. I watch our brave
sailor boy stifle his cry of knowledge
as the boat takes fatal water, then Ned's stricken face,
scanning the basalt waves
for what will never be seen again except in dreams.

All this was a long time ago, I remember.
None of them was drowned except me
whom a commotion of years washes over.
They hail me from the dream, they call an old man
to come aboard, these youths on an azure bay.
The waters may keep the dead, as the earth may,
and fire and air. But dream is my element.
Though I am still a strong swimmer
I can feel this channel widen as I swim.

II. Trelawny at Sompting, 1879

Sometimes I dream about those two cauldrons—
the one at Port Louis wherein I placed
the ruby-spangled Arab with my heart.
After the oil and camphor and ambergris,
the dark smoke rose and I sprang forward,
falling on the sand so near the fire
my hands were burned; and the one I had forged
at Leghorn, the iron machine for Ned and Shelley.
Shelley's brain seethed and bubbled but the heart
would not burn—a bright flame stroked and stroked it,
occasioned by a liquid still flowing from it,
and I took it in my hand to examine it,
after shrinking it in sea water, yet

it was still so hot as to burn my hand badly.
The day before, Ned Williams' handkerchief,
whole silk beside his exhumed carrion,
made Byron say, 'The entrails of a worm
hold together longer than the potters' clay
of which man is made.' During the burning,
he swam far out to sea.
                                        If I told Miss Taylor now
to leave the tea things and go gather faggots
and set them under my tub, I could rejoin them,
Zela, Arabian bird, and restless Shelley.

III. In the Protestant Cemetery

How did their lives go out from those deaths,
Keats' at the foot of the Spanish Steps, Shelley's
in the wild wave, accepted on the beach at Leghorn,
frail heroes, riding for sixty years the dreams
of Severn and Trelawny. How did their lives survive?

Who does not envy the young dead? Every year
the odds increase against accomplishment.
There is a thinning out, a dilution. The old
are in desperate trouble. These did not lose their models.

The great old man Severn was painting in Rome
when Trelawny in Sussex wrote to Clare, 'I have
an icy cold bath every morning and then go out
with my shirtsleeves tucked up and work in the garden.'
When they left that century it grew old.

Middle-aged people raised a subscription
to lay the old painter next to his young friend.
The adventurer followed, having lately written
a letter to Rome: 'In the year 1822 I purchased
a piece of land from the then Custodian—
I believe your father—under the pyramid
of Caius Cestius. I deposited the ashes
of my Friend Shelley in the one tomb
and the other I left for my ashes . . .'

We are parodies of boys and girls and we're aging.
After thirty who can think of himself except
as foully wronged, only the satiric overtones vary.
Judging ourselves harshly for natural losses,
we throw ourselves with less and less confidence
on the charity of our youth. We need good examples,
we need these two old men here under the cypresses.

Grace

For Dr. Langou

I. Surgery

When they needed a foreign part,
a valve which was not to be found
or spared elsewhere in his ample,
useful body, they chose a pig's valve.

This will be compatible, they reasoned,
with such pig-headed machinery
as has maintained a minor poet
for sixty-three years in America.

II. Convalescence

Once a week on Thursday there's a *souk*
or open market in Salé, the old Roman port
facing Rabat across the Bou Regreg.
At least one dentist always sets up shop—
a table of gunmetal teeth, formerly human.
One day I saw a woman have one pulled,
or saw as much as a queasy heart could watch.
The *chirurgien dentiste* was a small man,
authoritative, Berber I think.
His left foot was set gently on the woman's
shoulder, and when I last looked,
difficult, silent progress was being made.
A concept of necessary suffering, praise Allah,
is common to all civilizations.

Soon I will need to imagine again
what she was feeling, but for a few more days
that will not be necessary, a sensation
my body was too fastidious to wait for
hovers inside me. Even mortality
is briefly imaginable, like pain.
Arab sister, in your dark-robed dignity,
may we both be healed of our cures and live
painlessly forever, as our bodies urge.

III. Grace

Growing older, I totter into the lists
of the religious, tilt.

(Finally, you will have to look me up
in the joust of modern poets
where my pen name, *Lancelittle,*
may not yet have appeared
or already have been expunged,
as the listless spectators mewl,
Waste them, waste them. Whoever they are.)

To have been saved by the prayers
of friends, or by Panache,
one of God's servants, may come
to the same thing, a religious thing.

(Me who have congratulated myself
on cunning diagnoses and incisions,
though the sonnets or whoever they were
tended later to die
of unforeseen complications.)

The list of those who make acceptable prayer
endures. Though printed, contrary
to their express wish, in gold
and mother-of-pearl, it is not tacky.

(Names in all directories save this one
come and go, the jousters unhorsed,
accomplishments and what were taken
for accomplishments trotting away,
their reins at trail. Under the bleachers,
in programs the courtiers keep dropping,
the names are still legible but who reads them?)

I am glad for some who had not wasted grace
on the superstitious man, the apprentice,
but could master it—perhaps in the person
of Panache, the surgeon—to restore

a faint, fibrillating organ, lapsed
but Christian, starting everything up again.

A Note about the Author

William Meredith was born in New York City in 1919, was graduated from Princeton University in 1940, and served as a naval aviator during the Second World War and the Korean War. His first book of poems, *Love Letter from an Impossible Land*, was chosen by Archibald MacLeish for the Yale Series of Younger Poets prize in 1944; the title poem had been written the year before in the Aleutian Islands. *Ships and Other Figures,* his second book of verse, was published by Princeton in 1948. *The Open Sea and Other Poems* (1958), *The Wreck of the Thresher and Other Poems* (1964), *Earth Walk: New and Selected Poems* (1970), *Hazard, the Painter* (1975), *The Cheer* (1980), and *Partial Accounts: New and Selected Poems* (1987), which won the Pulitzer Prize in Poetry, were all published by Alfred A. Knopf. Meredith is the editor of *Shelley: Selected Poems* (1962) and *Poets of Bulgaria* (1986). His translation of Guillaume Apollinaire's *Alcools: Poems 1889–1913* appeared in 1964.

William Meredith has won three of *Poetry*'s annual prizes, fellowships from the Guggenheim and Ford Foundations, the Brandeis Medal, and the Loines Award from the American Academy and Institute of Arts and Letters, of which he became a member in 1968. From 1964 through 1989 he was a chancellor of the Academy of American Poets; he currently serves the academy as a chancellor emeritus. In 1978 Meredith was appointed consultant in poetry to the Library of Congress, a position he held through 1980. He was awarded the 1980 International Vaptsarov Prize in Poetry, and in 1989 received a senior fellowship from the National Endowment for the Arts. He has taught at Princeton, the University of Hawaii, Middlebury College, Bread Loaf School of English, Bread Loaf Writers' Conference, and Carnegie Mellon University, but has been primarily associated with Connecticut College since 1955.

William Meredith lives in Uncasville, Connecticut with his companion of twenty-five years, Richard Harteis, but travels frequently to Bulgaria, where he was made a citizen by presidential decree in 1996.